BOOTSTRAPS NEED BOOTS

▼

It's all right to tell a man to lift himself

by his own bootstraps,

but it is a cruel jest to say to a bootless man that

he ought to lift himself by his own bootstraps.

MARTIN LUTHER KING JR.

▲

Hugh Segal

Bootstraps NEED Boots

One Tory's Lonely Fight to End Poverty in Canada

WITH A FOREWORD BY ANDREW COYNE

a UBC Press imprint
Vancouver . Toronto

27 26 25 24 23 22 21 20 19   5 4 3 2 1

Printed in Canada on FSC-certified ancient-forest-free paper (100% post-consumer recycled) that is processed chlorine- and acid-free.

Cataloguing data available from Library and Archives Canada.

ISBN 978-0-7748-9045-8 (hardcover)
ISBN 978-0-7748-9047-2 (PDF)
ISBN 978-0-7748-9048-9 (EPUB)
ISBN 978-0-7748-9049-6 (Kindle)

Canadä

UBC Press gratefully acknowledges the financial support for our publishing program of the Government of Canada (through the Canada Book Fund), the Canada Council for the Arts, and the British Columbia Arts Council.

Printed and bound in Canada by Friesens
Interior design: Irma Rodriguez
Set in TheSans and Myriad by Artegraphica Design Co. Ltd.
Substantive editor: Barbara Pulling
Copy editor: Deborah Kerr
Proofreader: Helen Godolphin
Indexer: Sergey Lobachev
Author photo on cover: Milan Ilnyckyj

Every effort has been made to identify, credit appropriately, and obtain publication rights for the photographs in this book. Notice of any errors or omissions will be gratefully received and correction made in subsequent editions.

UBC Press
The University of British Columbia
2029 West Mall
Vancouver, BC V6T 1Z2
www.ubcpress.ca

▼
▼
▼

To SADYE (DANKNER) SEGAL (1917–74),
my loving and patient mother,
who explained the real truth about the missing toy box

and

To the HONOURABLE DAVID SAMUEL HORN MACDONALD,
saxophone player, United Church minister,
member of Parliament, minister of the Crown,
Canadian food relief coordinator during the Ethiopian famine,
former ambassador to Addis Ababa,
my first boss in Canadian politics, and
the best friend and mentor one could ever have.

Contents

Foreword

ANDREW COYNE

"Why would a life-long Conservative," asks Hugh Segal in his preface, "support a guaranteed income?" His answer, in this engaging book – part autobiography, part apologia – is that there is no contradiction between the two, for which Segal's own life story is perhaps the best evidence.

No one reading Segal's affecting account of his upbringing on the "cheery edge of poverty" could come away with the belief that his interest in the issue is anything less than sincere, or personal. No one with any familiarity with his long career in politics and public service could likewise doubt the depth of his commitment to the Conservative and indeed the conservative cause, even as a child of the working poor and grandson of a union activist.

And yet there is a note of wistfulness in the telling. For Segal's brand of conservatism – humane, optimistic, as committed to spreading opportunity as to cutting taxes – is seemingly on the way out. And the other great cause of his life, the basic or guaranteed annual income, seems scarcely closer to being realized than when it first seized his imagination as an idealistic nineteen-year-old, fifty years ago.

From the 1969 Conservative "thinkers" conference that introduced the future senator to the idea, to the 1971 report of the Special Senate Committee on Poverty, to the Macdonald Royal Commission in the 1980s, to recent pilot projects in Ontario and elsewhere, the concept of a basic income guarantee – a radical simplification and rationalization of existing income support policies into a single unconditional transfer – has not lacked for high-powered enthusiasts. Indeed, it is often noted that it has support across the political spectrum: though often linked with the left, an early and influential proponent was the libertarian economist Milton Friedman.

Supporters on the left tend to emphasize its potential to ensure that no one in need goes without – for lack of ability to navigate the sometimes complex tangle of federal and provincial assistance programs. Supporters on the right focus more on its capacity to lower the "welfare wall," the confiscatory marginal tax rates implied by the dollar-for-dollar withdrawal of assistance many provincial welfare programs impose as recipients start to earn income – effectively punishing them for working.

If instead everyone were guaranteed a basic income, gradually reduced in line with their earnings, it might be possible to tackle the twin evils of poverty and dependence simultaneously. As Segal writes, a basic income program "can generate more genuine help, an increased incentive to work, and less waste, bureaucracy, and stigma than inadequate and overly rules-based welfare programs now provide."

But if the idea has widespread support, it has an equally wide range of detractors. On the right, many view the notion of providing people with a modest stipend, whether they work or not, as a disincentive to effort – as if the disincentives in the present system were not far worse. On the left, any talk of replacing existing programs is viewed with suspicion, whether out of fear that the net result would be a reduction in support to the poor or that fewer people would be employed in providing it.

But perhaps the most formidable opposition comes from those well-meaning souls in the middle, who fret that a basic income fails to get at the "root causes" of poverty. It is on this point that Segal makes his most cogent, and passionate, contribution, drawing on a lifetime of observation and research.

Poverty, he insists, is the cause, rather than the consequence, of multiple social pathologies, from ill health, to poor school performance, to family breakdown, to crime and drug abuse. If people are too poor "to pay their rent or put food on the table," the immediate need is not to spend precious time debating all the reasons why this might be so, or deciding whether they are deserving or undeserving. It's to make them less poor.

The "poverty is complex" school of thought, he writes, "is really the 'do nothing' school of thought. No state, however flush with excess cash, can address all the endless lists of causes that contribute to poverty – hence, invoking that complex myriad of causes is actually the tribal call for inertia." At best, it "assumes there are programmatic responses to poverty that can defeat it: a better designed housing subsidy, well-supplied food banks, or enhanced training programs. Yet the central issue for the poor is lack of money."

So, give them more of it. Don't wrap them up in a lot of red tape and load them up with a lot of services other people think they need. Give them money, and let them decide how best they can use it. That's the radical, revolutionary premise of the basic income: people with more money tend to be less poor.

Radical, and yet also ... conservative. "Reforming welfare," Segal writes, "so that those in need are topped up financially and thereby encouraged to work and improve their circumstances without being judged, demeaned, diminished, or micromanaged by the 'swells' who work in various overseeing government departments strikes me as the ultimate liberating and uplifting conservative instrument."

Of course, when people say they support or oppose a basic income guarantee, they often have very different ideas of what they mean. The details are critical: how high or low to make the base level of support, how sharply or gradually to withdraw it, whether to send everyone a cheque in the same amount then tax it back (sometimes called the "demogrant" approach), or whether the payment should vary with income, i.e., those above a certain level paying in and those below drawing out (the so-called "negative income tax").

Likewise, while some see a basic income as a replacement for a wide variety of existing programs – not just income support, but other social benefits currently delivered in kind – others see it essentially as a supplement to them. Depending on how all these questions are answered, the program can be depicted as either a wildly unaffordable bit of utopianism or a practical scheme to eliminate poverty (at modest additional expense).

What we do know is how it has worked in those areas where it has already been implemented. The combination of Old Age Security and the Guaranteed Income Supplement amounts to a basic income for seniors. Since the introduction of these programs in the 1960s and 1970s, poverty among the elderly, once endemic, has all but disappeared. Similarly, the federal Canada Child Benefit, a 2016 reform rationalizing a number of existing tax credits and income support programs for parents into a single, income-tested (and more generous) benefit, cut the incidence of child poverty by a third in just two years.

What remains, to fill in the gap, is a basic income for those of working age. Admittedly the arithmetic here is daunting, given the larger numbers involved. It will not be easy to put a decent floor under incomes, preserve work incentives, and keep the whole thing affordable. In a federation like Canada, there is also the difficulty of getting both the federal government and the provinces on board, working together rather than, as they so often do, at cross purposes: another historic obstacle to reform.

A universal basic income will probably not arrive at one stroke, but in the same incremental fashion that has been successful to date. It will take much experimentation, most likely at the provincial level. As the former Parliament Hill staffer and federal leadership candidate wryly observes in these pages, Ottawa will "never be the main source of real anti-poverty reform, since the urgent would always take precedence over the truly important in an unduly media-driven town."

Segal's particular contribution to this has been his design of the Ontario basic income pilot project, a three-year, three-city experiment implemented under the province's former Liberal government. He is justifiably outraged that it should have been cancelled, just a year after it started, by the incoming Conservative government of Doug Ford – not least given the legacy of progressive reforms (including a guaranteed income supplement for seniors) pioneered by previous Ontario Conservative governments, in which Segal had served.

And yet he remains an incurable optimist, the original "happy warrior," ever cheerful even in the face of adversity – personal or political. In this, as in his decades of commitment to bettering the lot of the poorest among us, conservatives would do well to follow his example.

Preface

▼

We cannot solve our problems with the
same thinking we used when we created them.

ALBERT EINSTEIN

▲

IN JUNE 2008, I was a keynote speaker at a conference in Dublin sponsored by the Basic Income Earth Network, a gathering of academics, community workers, anti-poverty advocates, priests, nuns, and activists on housing, pensions, health care, and food security from many countries in Europe, North and South America, and beyond. I was invited because of my decades-long championing of a new approach to welfare and poverty abatement known as a basic income, or guaranteed annual income. The idea, with proponents and opponents on both the left and the right, had consistently hit huge roadblocks in almost every finance ministry in the free world.

In my speech, I reflected on the extent to which being on the centre-right of Canadian politics while also being a determined life-long advocate for a basic income has had its moments of discomfort, particularly in the conservative circles that have defined my political life. At that time, the alliance between members of the Reform Party and remnants of the Progressive Conservative Party was, though polite, deeply inhospitable to any real approach to welfare reform.

I put it this way: "For more than thirty years, I have been a cheerful, if lonely, Conservative proponent in Canada for a guaranteed annual income or a basic income floor." My listeners, assembled in the rather large lecture hall of the University of Dublin's business school, looked bemused, sympathetic, or curious – the way you might look when you see someone walk absent-mindedly into a telephone pole.

Before I was to speak, I'd had coffee with Father Sean Healy, a delightful and obviously warm-hearted Jesuit priest. "So, you're a conservative senator, are you?" he said to me. "And you care about the poor? How very interesting. Well, good luck to you." Expressed in various ways by associates in business, fellow directors on for-profit and not-for-profit boards, journalists and columnists of the left, right, and centre, and parliamentarians of differing stripes, the good father's reaction has been a steady part of my life since 1969. That was when, as a young Progressive Conservative (PC), I was introduced to a new concept, a means to lift poor Canadians into the economy in a way that was humane, respectful, and affordable. A basic income floor had been proposed at a PC "seminal thinkers" conference in Niagara Falls that year, as a better way to protect equality of opportunity for all Canadians. Better, at least, than the patchwork of federal, provincial, and municipal programs, supplemented by charitable and church-based activity, that was complex, wasteful, and most importantly, unsuccessful at helping people get out of poverty and creating a genuine fair point of departure. The PC Party, fresh from an electoral defeat at the hands of the charismatic Pierre Trudeau, was licking its wounds at the time, regrouping and reflecting under the able, sensible, and profoundly decent leadership of Robert Stanfield, its newly chosen leader. Convinced by what I heard, I have advanced the idea of a basic income at every opportunity since then.

This book is not an argument for the nuances of one social program over another. Rather, it attempts to answer the question that I have been asked so often over the years. Why would a life-long Conservative support a guaranteed income? The conservative and Conservative wheelhouse is about lower taxes, less government, and preserving what is best. It generally avoids social and economic policy change. So what could drive a Conservative who had run for office and served premiers and prime ministers as an advisor, organizer, and senior official to champion this radical shift in how we structure our societies and economies?

How dare he set aside the "survival of the fittest" precept that drove many European, American, and Canadian conservatives?

In 2016, my third year as principal of Massey College, I accepted an assignment to prepare a detailed discussion paper for the Province of Ontario on how a basic income might be tested through a carefully planned pilot project. At my explicit request, it was a pro-bono assignment.

For the next three months, I devoted the better part of weekends, evenings, and non-existent summer holidays to this task. Working with Maripier Isabelle, who was completing her doctorate in health economics at the University of Toronto, I attended a series of roundtables, panels, and meetings. These involved provincial and municipal officials in Ottawa and Toronto, advocacy groups, folks living in poverty themselves, and federal public servants in the numerous ministries working on various aspects of social policy, statistical measurement, intergovernmental cooperation, health, and finance. All in all, there were close to a hundred meetings and phone conferences, each one focused on how best to design the pilot for a basic income. We held discussions with other provinces and with the other two parties in the Ontario legislature as well.

My discussion paper, published by the Province of Ontario in November 2016, laid out one approach to how such a pilot might be designed to determine whether a basic income grant made more sense than the existing welfare and disability support programs in terms of both outcomes for the recipients and the net cost to the province. The government decided to launch a three-year pilot project in Thunder Bay, Hamilton, and Lindsay, following many of the recommendations in the discussion paper. Participant recruitment began in the spring of 2017. Sadly, even though four thousand people had been recruited, the entire effort was cancelled in July 2018 by the newly elected Progressive Conservatives. This was a shocking breach of faith by the government, and it signalled the desertion of any commitment whatsoever to an evidence-based, decision-making approach to welfare reform.

Despite the abandonment of the pilot program, the deeply informative and highly constructive process of assembling the discussion paper underlined for me even more strongly that not trying something different – not even attempting to see if poverty can be alleviated in a more humane and efficient way – is a very serious mistake. The only thing worse than a bias shaped by poor expectations about low-income citizens and their prospects is a sense of complacent defeatism about how, as a mature and productive society, we can reduce poverty and its impact. There was little doubt in my mind – a mind shaped by this issue since my nineteenth birthday – that the present approach to welfare and poverty abatement was economically unproductive, extremely discouraging of work and social engagement, and intrinsically unaffordable.

I would like to think that, had I been raised in a family where economic security and future prospects were never in doubt, good sense and genuine public engagement would have brought me to the same conclusions regarding an income guarantee for all. Certainly, the difficult economic circumstances of my early life made me responsive to this central idea, and my dedication to it has merely increased through years of work in politics, business, and academe.

Policy change, especially one as fundamental as the creation of a basic income guarantee for all, should not be easy to achieve in a democracy as pluralist and diverse as Canada's. But nor should this be impossible simply because it is hard. Frank discussion across political lines will be necessary to pave the way. Why not put partisanship aside and use the evidence we have had for decades about poverty, at home and abroad, to structure a modern effort to alleviate it, here and around the world? My own conservatism – and mainstream conservatism itself, for that matter – has never been about preserving class privilege. It is about broadening the economic mainstream by affording genuine equality of opportunity to those who are outside the circle. It is in that spirit, with a blend of humility and optimism, that I reflect here on where and why I developed such a strong bias for a basic income guarantee.

HUGH SEGAL
Charleston Lake
Ontario

BOOTSTRAPS NEED BOOTS

CHAPTER 1

The Cheery Edge of Poverty

▼

The capitalist version of the politics
of inevitability – the market as a substitute for
policy – generates economic inequality that
undermines belief in progress.

TIMOTHY SNYDER, *THE ROAD TO UNFREEDOM*

▲

I WAS THE LAST of three boys (we were a boys-only brood, much to my mother's disappointment) born to Sadye Dankner and Morris Jack Segal, who were married in 1937 in Montreal. Mom was the eldest sister in a family of six children. Her parents, Benjamin Dankner and Rose Kauffman, emigrated to Canada from the eastern Austro-Hungarian Empire in the late 1890s. Benjamin and Rose started Dankner's Bakery on Boulevard St. Laurent, which continued successfully for many years despite being ravaged by the Depression and some tension with the unions. My grandparents, my uncles and aunts, and my mother lived, classically, over the store, and all of them worked or helped in the bakery, which was open from Sunday mornings until Friday at noon. My grandparents were Orthodox Jews, who always closed for the Sabbath.

I did not meet my maternal grandfather, because he died in 1942 of complications from diabetes. But I heard many stories about him. The one that particularly stuck with me poignantly recounted an interesting aspect of the seven-day period of mourning (shiva) following his death. My mother told me that every day, those who came to pay their respects to the widow and children would leave envelopes containing money (uncharacteristically, since this is not a Jewish tradition). The accompanying notes all said something to the effect of "We had no money during the Depression. Mr. Dankner said we should take what bread we needed to help feed our family, and we could settle up when things were better. We never did settle up, but we should now." The Dankners were not poor when my grandfather died, but neither were they rich. They were always struggling business owners in the labour-intensive world of a small kosher retail bakery in the centre of Canada's Eastern European immigrant community.

My dad was the son of Benjamin Segal and Hudja Soifer, refugees who came to Montreal after the First World War from what was then Communist Russia. My grandfather had been a tailor in a town called Mogilev Podolsk, near Minsk, where the family lived in a tiny house with a dirt floor and outdoor plumbing. He himself came to Montreal before the war ended and worked and saved to bring his family to join him.

In czarist and Communist Russia, they had been very poor. Their diet was barely subsistence, relying more on cornmeal mush *(mamiliga)*, potatoes, and beets than on any regular protein. Bits of herring were a rare treat. My grandfather had supported the Menshevik side of the anti-czarist movement and had decided that the carnage of the Russo-Japanese War, the grinding poverty, and the regular pogroms under the czar were a compelling reason to leave. The near-starvation conditions and regular pogroms most weeks in his village offered absolutely no prospects for his children.

He came to Montreal by ship via Halifax, with the assistance of the Baron de Hirsch society (named for its benefactors Baron and Baroness Maurice and Clara de Hirsch) to find a place to live and a job in a tailor shop. His goal was to save enough money to bring over my grandmother and their children, of which my dad was one, along with his sisters, one older and one younger – my aunts Rose and Gertie.

On his first attempt, the money and tickets he shipped to his family were stolen in transit. He then worked through a local MP to make a second attempt via the British mission in Minsk. (Canada had no independent foreign offices outside Washington and London until after

1931 and the Statute of Westminster.) This second dispatch arrived safely, and his family set sail for Halifax in 1920.

As family legend has it, when he went to the Montreal train station to meet them – now an employed resident of a growing Canadian city, with income, an icebox filled with food, and a warm-water flat with both heat and indoor facilities – he looked so prosperous, well fed, and robust that they did not recognize him.

My grandfather worked hard to earn a living and deal with the costs of raising three children. Although he spoke only Russian and Yiddish at first, and had a wife who suffered from chronic kidney disease because of her many years of hunger in Russia, he was resolute and always cheery. Unlike my maternal grandparents, my grandfather Ben was not terribly religious. His disposition was to appreciate and adapt to his surroundings. He identified with the plight of working men and women who, like himself, had only piecework, unpredictable wages, and no benefits of any kind with which to negotiate the larger world.

I knew Benjamin Segal as a doting and engaged grandfather. Visits from Zaida or, later, to his apartment in the Côte-des-Neiges district of Montreal, were a regular part of life, always enjoyable and always a chance to learn a little from a person of long years and varied experience. Sadly, I never knew Hudja, his first wife and my paternal grandmother, though family lore made it clear that I owed my very inception to her kindly suggestion to my parents that two children were simply not enough. As my mom had always wanted a girl, this idea did not meet stiff resistance.

My two older brothers were born five years apart: Seymour in 1939 and Brian in 1944. *Faute de mieux*, I arrived in October 1950, a strapping five-pound, seven-ounce little boy. Hudja had died earlier that year of kidney failure, the kind that poverty and malnourishment can produce. I was named after her, as is the tradition in some faiths and cultures.

By the time I was born into a very low-end, working-class family in what is now called Le Plateau, my maternal grandfather had died. My maternal grandmother would die fifteen years later, in 1956. They were only in their sixties, both ravaged by diseases for which we now have life-extending therapies.

At the time of my birth, Benjamin Segal was helping to set up the revivified International Ladies' Garment Workers' Union (ILGWU) local through a strike of the Cloakmakers' local, in whose ranks he had risen to shop steward. Surnames such as Shane, Dubinsky, Kirzner, and Jodoin, senior organizers from Quebec, Montreal, and New York, were often mentioned around the family table. In the days before the ILGWU, cutters, tailors, sewers, and cloakmakers were paid by the garment, with no guaranteed weekly salary and zero benefits. The first strike my grandfather led was the result of an owner announcing on a Tuesday that if output did not double by quitting time on Friday, all the workers would be fired. As meeting the deadline was both impossible and unreasonable, my grandfather led his co-workers into the street. "We walk out like human beings today or we crawl out like mice on Friday night," he said to them. His union loyalty was not about class warfare or a dictatorship of the proletariat. His experience with Russian communism had cured him of any interest in those excesses. His involvement was simply about dignity and self-respect for the men and women who, despite working hard every day, could not make ends meet or build better lives for their families.

This was the sort of stuff on which I was raised. Combine it with stories about my maternal grandfather helping the less fortunate customers of Dankner's Bakery during the tough Depression years, and you get the general drift.

There was also a mild but pronounced class distinction between my maternal and paternal families. The Dankner-Kauffman crowd came from a slightly better-off area in Eastern Europe. They owned a business and were of Orthodox stock. In addition, they had arrived earlier than the Segals. Late arrivals were viewed as "green" or "greener" in the Yiddish dialect. As well, those who were modestly merchant or middle class, however they might be struggling, had great disdain for those who were even more modest and working class in status. My father often joked that he had had to play pinochle with Rose Dankner for what seemed like years before he was permitted to date her daughter.

That class distinction held for generations. My mother's brothers and sisters either became entrepreneurs themselves or married Americans and worked with them in small businesses that were quite successful. My maternal uncles had finished high school, had start-up jobs at the family bakery, and moved in relatively successful economic circles. Through hard work, they started businesses in the ladies' lingerie manufacturing field (Montreal) and retail baking and furniture – the latter two in Rochester,

New York: Quality Kosher Bakery and Fitch Furniture, both on Joseph Avenue. During the Rochester race riots of late July 1964, when many stores were looted and destroyed, both the bakery and the furniture store were left untouched. My uncles had black employees and worked hard to ensure that all customers were treated with equal respect, including the extension of credit as required.

My mom's youngest brother, Max, lied about his age to join the Canadian army in 1939 and became a member of the Princess Louise Dragoon Guards. He landed on the coast of Sicily and fought up the spine of Italy with the Canadian Forces in 1943–44. Despite serious wounds in the Italian campaign, he recuperated sufficiently to be part of the liberation of Holland with his Canadian comrades. When he returned to Montreal, he applied for work with the Quebec Provincial Police, now the Sûreté du Québec. He had handled guns and been a motorcycle dispatch rider in Holland. But because he had fought in "la guerre des Anglais" and was Jewish, the recruiting officer, though not unpleasant, found his pursuit of a police job quite idiotic. Max went on to become a successful sales and manufacturing player in the women's millinery business in Montreal, which suited his personality and demonstrated his gumption.

My dad had no such luck. When he arrived in Canada, he spoke neither English nor French. He was put into Grade 1 at Edward VII Public School at the age of ten. Embarrassed because his classmates were so much younger, he was desperate to leave school and get a job. There was always some grinding need at home. He left school in Grade 6, found work sweeping up in a garment-manufacturing company, and progressed to shipping and other menial, go-nowhere positions. When my oldest brother was born, my father received a two-dollar-a-week raise.

Long periods of unemployment, a personal bankruptcy, and a failed effort on my father's part to be a travelling men's shirt salesman conspired to make our financial position quite precarious and sometimes desperate. There was no unemployment insurance or medicare in the late 1950s and early 1960s.

I was barely ten years old and did not fully understand the dynamics of our financial instability. Our home was always warm, and we seemed to have all the food we needed – and then some. But certain intrusions heralding a financial collapse were hard to ignore. We lived in a second-floor walk-up in lower Outremont, part of a classic Montreal working-class triplex with outside stairs, and were always behind on our rent. One day, a bailiff arrived and repossessed our car. On a second visit, our furniture was seized, both of which had an impact. Mom had stayed home to raise her three children, but when Dad became unemployed, she took a job at an all-night drugstore.

While my brothers were in high school, they worked as cashiers at Steinberg's, the supermarket on Côte-des-Neiges and Queen Mary. This did not seem unusual for working-class folks. That all of their earnings went to pay family expenses, with none set aside for university, did strike me as unfair. Many working-class families experienced similar or worse financial and part-time work pressures.

One event that made a lasting impression on me was a visit to Belmont Amusement Park in Montreal's northwest Cartierville suburb, two streetcar rides away. My brother Seymour decided to treat me, using his cashier's earnings to pay for our excursion. We spent a perfect day, enjoying rides and cotton candy. I was exhausted and delighted at this very infrequent luxury for an edge-of-poverty working-class kid. But my brother caught pure hell from my parents when we came home that afternoon because his earnings had not gone to the household coffers. This was not easy for me to understand, at least not at nine years of age, and it was something I would never forget.

In areas of east-end Montreal or at Point St. Charles, there were many working-class families that were far poorer than the Segals, and we would talk about them around the supper table. I attended a private, fee-based religious school that taught the curriculum of the Protestant School Board of Greater Montreal for half a day and classic Hebrew language, Bible study, theology, history, and literature for the other half. I could afford to attend only because my great-uncle on my mother's side of the family, Ben Beutel, was a well-off manufacturer of men's suits (Premier Brand Suits), a noted philanthropist, and the pro-bono chair of my school. He paid my fees. My hand-me-down clothes were not all that bad, despite the fact that I was chubbier than either of my brothers at the same age. But extra funds for school trips, gym clothes, and the rest were always a struggle and produced great machinations at home.

As I rounded the corner into adolescence, some impressions had begun to set in. I realized that poor people had far fewer choices than everyone else. That money pressures took their toll: on relationships, on outlook, on day-to-day life, on parental harmony, and on future prospects. That how well off or connected your parents or grandparents were made a huge difference. That working hard mattered, but it was not always enough. That disadvantage was a scale reflected in your relationships with the people you knew, related or otherwise, who were doing either better or worse. That sometimes even people of modest means had to help those who were worse off – and there were always folks who were worse off. That fairness did not come naturally in a society where everyone was trying to get ahead. Sometimes those at the bottom of the ladder had to make noise so that more people could step on and hope to step up.

None of this seemed even remotely political. I understood things very much at the family level. Cousins my age lived in detached homes in lovely districts and had two cars and wondrous toys (my Rochester cousin Neal possessed a Ride-em red tractor, rarely shared). When I asked for a small plastic rubber-tire Imperial Oil truck hanging on the toy rack at the local drugstore, I was scolded. This was not about genuine deprivation. It was about learning, from a very young age, that "we can't afford it" was the usual answer to questions about getting or doing something that others next door or in our family always had or did.

Millions of children have experienced worse. After all, we lived in Montreal, then Canada's premier city. Streets were safe. School was safe. We could worship freely in our own faith. On Saturday nights, we could watch les Canadiens play hockey, sitting in front of our own twelve-inch Philco television (the set came to us because our uncle Hy Fitelson, married to my mother's sister Ceal, was the proprietor of Fitch Furniture in Rochester). My childhood was not about despair. It was about getting a strong sense of where you stood and about what you did or did not have the right to hope for.

Being on the cheery edge of poverty is not, as some bootstraps proponents assert, about building character and ambition. It is about understanding that the financial insecurity at the centre of your existence, once installed in your memory bank, never leaves. And since you don't live in abject poverty, it's also about realizing how much worse the feelings of instability and insecurity must be for those who do.

CHAPTER 2

The Missing Toy Box

▼

We are not rich by what we possess,

but by what we can do without.

EMMANUEL KANT

▲

AT THE AGE OF NINE, you don't have many possessions that are deeply important. My little bedroom, off the kitchen and beside the furnace room, was fine. It had a single bed, a bright, if threadbare, rug, and a small closet. It was not far from our second-floor balcony, which over-looked the back laneway that we shared with other triplexes and four-plexes in the neighbourhood. We lived in lower Outremont, on Avenue de l'Épée, near Lajoie. In the back alley, we played street hockey and wall tennis, bouncing the ball off the stucco walls. Trucks sometimes drove up the lane, delivering coal (later, oil) to our basements. We enjoyed playing "cowboys and Indians" or hide and seek in the lanes that connected de l'Épée to Bloomfield and the cross-street at Lajoie. It was a happy place, where kids could play outside all afternoon until called to dinner.

The central "altar" of my bedroom was a mahogany toy box about five feet tall. Its large lidded compartment served as a seat. It held many toys, from stuffed teddy bears, small trucks, and cap guns to a constructed Davy Crockett hat. We couldn't afford a real Davy Crockett hat with the faux-raccoon tail, so mine had a cloth tail in a greyish tone. There were soldiers made of pipe cleaners, Dinky Toy cars, several Slinkies, and some colouring books and pencil crayons. There was a whistle on a cord for hockey games, a small bat and a baseball, a bolo bat, and a Tonka tractor that I especially loved. The box also contained a series of cereal box submarines that were magically powered by baking powder (the original non-polluting fuel?). I had a small three-car pull train made of wood (alas, more than fifty years of asking for an electric train has been futile), along with a skipping rope or two, and some street chalk. Not, perhaps, wealth in objective terms, but it was my little treasure trove. The back of the box was carved in the shape of a beaver, and it had brass pegs from which to hang coats, bathrobes, peaked hockey hats (vaunting the Canadiens, of course), and scarves.

I don't remember where it came from – a hand-me-down from a wealthier relative? Something given to me from my grandparents' house? I'm not sure. But it was my home base. For me, it was like today's desktop or laptop computer or CPU. I could leave schoolbooks on the seat or hide stuff in the secret compartment. The toy box was at least as important as my bed, though not as important as the fridge just around the corner in our large eat-in kitchen, replete with its chrome-legged arborite-topped table and soft plastic-upholstered chrome-framed chairs.

So my shock could not have been greater when I entered my room late one afternoon in the dead of winter to find all my stuff piled neatly against the wall and the toy box gone.

My dad was not at home, so I went to my brother Brian, who was fifteen and a student at Outremont High.

"Where is my toy box?" I asked accusingly.

"Dad had to use it for something," Brian said in an uncomfortable voice.

"When will I get it back?"

"Better ask Dad."

I was troubled, and at a loss. What could my unemployed father, out looking for work, want with my toy box? It made no sense.

Dad came home around 6:30 p.m., having stopped at the Steinberg's up the street for some groceries. I heard him come into the kitchen and start making supper. I put down my pipe cleaner men and wandered into the kitchen. My father expected the usual hug.

"Hi Touie," he said. "How was school?" (As a child, I could not pronounce the "H" in Hugh or Hughie, so my nickname became Touie.)

"Okay. Mr. Michaeli was sick, so we had a substitute teacher."

"Any good?" he asked.

"Her Hebrew had a different accent. Some said maybe Moroccan."

Dad was making patties, mixing ground beef with egg yolks, bread crumbs, and some mustard. Fried in a pan with onions, accompanied by mashed potatoes and green peas from a can, those patties were one of my favourite meals. My father was making dinner because my mom had already gone off to her nightshift job as a cashier at the Medical Arts Pharmacy at Guy and Sherbrooke, about a forty-five-minute bus ride away.

"Dad?" I started. "Could you –?"

He stopped me cold. "Touie, I gave your toy box away to the people upstairs on the third floor."

"The Lacroix family?" I asked, puzzled.

"They needed it for heat in the furnace."

"My toy box?" I began to cry.

"They had no money for the coal man. It's very cold outside – and their welfare cheque isn't due till the end of the month."

"So you gave them my toy box!"

"Had no choice, Touie. They asked for money. I had none to lend, so I figured they could burn the wood until they got some coal. The mahogany will burn slowly, the wood is really thick – it will help."

"Dad, that was my toy box!"

"We'll get you another one someday."

"When? Besides, it won't be the same."

I stomped off to my room and slammed the door. Anger, desolation, and despair (but mostly anger) flowed through my veins.

About twenty minutes later, Dad hollered, "Brian, Touie, supper!"

I stayed where I was. A few minutes later, Brian knocked on my door. "It's going to get cold."

"Not coming," I said with some flourish.

"Touie, it's your favourite! Schnitzel!" (For reasons that were never clear to me, my mother called this hamburger dish "schnitzel," but breaded second-cut veal was called "veal chops" – go figure.)

"Don't care, not coming!"

After he and Brian had finished eating, my dad brought a plate of food to my room, along with a glass of Eskimo Nectar (its actual brand name) ginger ale.

"Touie, here's some supper," he offered, knocking on my door.

I didn't answer.

He poked his head in. "Touie, have some supper. I promise to get you a toy box as soon as I find a job."

"It won't be the same, and I'm not hungry." The first part of this statement was an assertion, the second a lie. But I was determined to be angry and tough.

I fell asleep in my clothes and woke up at about 11:00 p.m. The hall was dark. Both my brothers were out, and I could hear my dad snoring. My parents' bedroom was past the bathroom and down the hall, near the dining room. It was far away, but his snoring had serious tonal depth and volume. I changed into my pyjamas and went back to bed, listening to the wind rattle the loose windowpane just a few inches from where my toy box used to be. I cried myself to sleep.

The next morning, as usual, Mom woke me up.

"Good morning, Touie. You have to catch the bus in an hour and fifteen."

I took a shower, brushed my teeth, combed my hair, and put on my thick wide-wale corduroy pants, a hand-me-down flannel shirt in shades of green, a red sleeveless sweater, and my Savage shoes. My breakfast routine involved cereal, frozen concentrated orange juice, a banana, and a huge tablespoon of the most foul-tasting cod liver oil in the world. I often tried to pour it into my orange juice to dilute the taste, but Mom would not allow it.

"Dilute the oil and it won't heal!" she would intone.

Brian and I sat quietly, listening to CJAD's Morning Show with Bill Roberts. Mom seemed preoccupied, and Dad had gone downtown already to talk to someone in a clothing factory about a job. After breakfast, I went to the furnace shed to put on my heavy flannel leggings, my duffle coat, and my brown vulcanized rubber buckle boots.

"Touie, I made you lunch," my mom called. "The cold schnitzel from last night will make great sandwiches. Don't forget to eat the celery, and don't eat the Dare cookies first."

I said nothing.

Mom joined me in the furnace shed. "I guess you skipped supper last night. Daddy told me."

"I wasn't hungry."

"Touie, you're always hungry! Why did you skip supper?"

No answer.

"Daddy said you were angry."

No answer.

"About your toy box."

Brian was putting on his boots to walk to Outremont High. He didn't have to wear leggings or take a bus to school. He left before my conversation with Mom continued.

Finally, I said, "He gave it away without my permission."

"Oh," said my mom. "Your permission."

"Yes."

"Young man" – it was never a good sign when she said that – "I am really disappointed in you."

"In me?"

"Yes, in you."

I began to tear up.

"Hugh David Segal" – also not a good sign – "you know where the box went."

"It was my toy box!"

"Touie, Mr. Lacroix had no money for heat, and Dad had no money to help. How do you think Mr. Lacroix felt, having to ask Daddy for help? How do you think Daddy felt, having nothing to give but a wooden box? And you're angry? I'm ashamed of you! How could you be so selfish?"

I walked out the door, holding my mom's hand, bawling my eyes out as we went up de l'Épée to Bernard. She got on the bus with me. I cried all the way down to boulevard St. Joseph and Park Avenue, where my school was located. It was the worst moment of my whole nine years.

I didn't understand why I was in trouble, when it was my toy box that had been burned.

I hadn't understood that there were people poorer than we in our triplex.

I didn't understand anyone telling me that the box really didn't matter. It mattered to me.

I did understand the guilt I felt for upsetting my mother.

Weeks passed. Whenever I was in my room, I thought about my toy box, now replaced by shopping bags full of my treasure.

About three months elapsed before I began to understand. No one could stand by, or should stand by, and see a neighbour go without something as basic as heat. I did not forgive my dad. But I began slowly to understand why what happened had happened.

This was the lesson that activated a nascent sense of conscience in me. Guilt is a powerful force.

▼

Conscience is many things: a sense of obligation; a sense of right and wrong. For me, after the sacrifice of my beloved toy box, my anger, and feeling of violation, conscience was a compelling sense of guilt at my selfishness. I learned how painful a motivation guilt could be. More importantly, I had learned that there were people living close by who were in rougher shape than my family. What might be a small luxury for one family could well be a survival necessity for another. All of this lodged somewhere in the place between soul and mind. But I still didn't forgive my dad!

This incident occurred before the health insurance breakthroughs of Saskatchewan premier Tommy Douglas became the norm throughout Canada. In those days, many immigrant communities founded sick and death benefit societies into which low-income people paid small amounts so that there might be a burial plot when they passed or a tiny bit of financial assistance when they got ill. My dad was a member of something called the King Edward Benefit Association (KEBA), which was similar to the groups set up by the Ukrainian, Polish, Chinese, Italian, Hungarian, and Greek communities during their first-generation years in Canada.

These organizations raised funds, sponsored communal events, elected executives, and generally sought to be a community-centred force for cooperative progress. The KEBA even had a bowling league that met at Sunset Lanes on rue de la Savane on Tuesday nights. My dad belonged to that league for many years. He quit only after my mom joined and won the Rookie of the Year Award, which meant she was a better five-pin bowler than he was.

Most of that was peripheral noise to a pre-teen. But I do remember the monthly KEBA meetings at the Moose Hall on Park Avenue near Laurier. My dad attended, and as the meetings followed my swimming lessons at the nearby YMHA, he took me along. After singing "God Save the Queen," the meeting dealt with its agenda. A dry-cleaning store owner by the name of Mr. Zangwell officiated as president, and others around the table reported in, asking questions and proposing motions. The Cemetery Committee report was always first, followed by the Bowling League Committee. Then there would be the Health and Sickness Report. Finally came the Distress Committee report.

This last report was about families or individuals who were in severe financial distress because of illness, accidents, business collapse, unemploy-ment, and the like. Their names were never mentioned, in respect for their privacy. The KEBA meeting decided how much money to give them, either as a gift or a one-time loan, classically called a "free loan" because no interest was ever charged and because payback was on an "as and if ready and able" basis. My father always argued in favour of generosity. Later, when he worked as a cab driver and had a little extra income, he donated to that committee. I was proud of him for that.

Everyone lowered his voice during this last part of the meeting. Being poor was embarrassing for the people in need. Those who were margin-ally, if temporarily, better off discussed their situation discreetly, in hushed tones. Sometimes, I wondered if my family's financial circumstances would become so dire that folks would talk about us in this way. When-ever I did, I thought about my toy box.

CHAPTER 3

Happiness, Anger, Religion, and Hockey

▼

Maturity is a high price to pay for growing up.

TOM STOPPARD

▲

AS THE THIRD CHILD in my family, and the baby, I received a lot of attention from my parents, brothers, aunts, uncles, and grandfather. School was mostly fun, and my private religious school had excellent teachers on both the religious and the secular public curriculum side. Children in poor economic straits often don't fully understand their circumstances. Motivated, encouraging parents, supportive siblings, and a constructive educational experience can create a reasonably cheery bubble for their daily life. The toy box event stands out in my mind precisely because it was unique. It was not part of an ongoing cycle of multiple incidents, such as many poor kids face, that create anger and loss and that shape attitudes and emotional responses for years to come.

Being in a religious school, attending services regularly, and beginning, at the age of eleven, to prepare for my bar mitzvah meant that I saw the world through the lens of the Old Testament. In my first-generation minority faith community, the parameters were defined by how and where you lived, the personalities of your teachers and fellow students, and the ups and downs of family life. We were well outside the main-stream of Montreal, of Quebec, and of Canada. This was not isolating; it simply was what it was.

With regard to our studies, our parents viewed anything less than an "A" in every subject, secular or religious, as a personal act of treason. Not much pressure at all! Both of my brothers were more athletically inclined than I was. Seymour played soccer at Baron Byng High School and baseball in a neighbourhood league. He became a very strong goalie in his teens, a position that inspired a love of hockey for many years. Brian played basketball and, though not six foot seven, was a very engaged and competitive player. In my case, the phys. ed. activities at United Talmud Torah academy were, shall we say, not great fun.

Being chubby didn't help. Both my brothers magically missed that physical attribute. Families of modest means sometimes have an instinctive tendency to over-serve at the dinner table. In our house, food was always plentiful, perhaps too much so.

My mom, the daughter of a baker, was not a slim woman. Her generation had a fashion sense that being large was healthy. My dad's impoverished Russian provenance meant he was attracted to that quality in my mother along with many other attributes. I still have photos of me as an infant, being held by my mother, in which I appear to be smaller than her forearm. After my birth, she had visited our family physician, Joe Goldberg, for advice on weight loss. She was a happy homemaker, subscribing to the culture of the time, and had not yet joined the workforce. Our family's economic circumstances, though tenuous at best, had not collapsed. It was 1951. Dr. Goldberg put her on a moderate diet and suggested that taking up smoking would help with appetite control. After that, she smoked a pack and a half of Rothman's filter tips every day. My dad smoked either Buckingham or Sportsmen's unfiltered. Both had well-textured morning coughs. My mom's was relatively mild, but my dad's had a "wake up the neighbourhood" tone and reach.

Alcohol was never an issue in our home. One bottle of Seagram's VO rye whisky and a bottle of Crown Royal, the latter to be served only when someone graduated, had a bar mitzvah, or died, would last for years. Wine was rarely at our table, except at Passover. Then we drank the dreadful, overly sweet wine made by a great-uncle-in-law, Frank Mendelsohn, who had married my mom's aunt Dora.

Food was our bridge over troubled waters: of rent in arrears, poor-paying jobs lost, drug and medical bills. Cleaning your plate was a way of proving your loyalty to the parents you loved and who loved you. Second-cut breaded veal chops, mashed potatoes, and canned peas (fresh vegetables were too expensive), served with bread and dill pickles, washed down by sugary ginger ale, and capped off with syrupy canned fruit (often peaches), were normal nightly fare. School lunches consisted of two salami sandwiches on rye with mustard, a stick of celery, Dare chocolate chip cookies, and sweetened apple juice. Before my dad became a cab driver, he parked our station wagon overnight at the Modern Garage on Bernard between de l'Épée and Hutchison. I often accompanied him for the five-minute drive to the garage because the fifteen-minute walk home generally featured a stop at the local depanneur for a Lowney's Cherry Blossom to be enjoyed with a glass of whole milk, or at least 2 percent, before bed. Food was a great elixir, and I was not an unwilling soldier in this consumptive battle.

At my school, I was not isolated in my chubbiness. And relatives responded positively. My mom took their regular comment – "Sadye, he looks well fed and healthy" – as a compliment. Every extra snack I ate was simply me doing my share. Family weddings and gatherings were judged by the food available and consumed. Quantity mattered as much, if not more, than quality. Most of my fellow students had at least one parent with immigrant roots in Eastern Europe or knew once-emaciated survivors of the concentration camps. Eating to excess was a way of proving that Hitler had not completely succeeded. So, mine was a home where loving and conscientious parents indulged in over-consumption of tobacco and large quantities of food.

We never discussed weight or a balanced lifestyle. Instead, we endlessly debated the virtues of noodle pudding (kugel) from Western Europe, sweet and mushy with raisins, versus the salty and crispy kugel of Russian-Polish food traditions.

I played hockey from ages nine to fourteen. Those five years saw me progress through the mosquito, peewee, and bantam levels of the Ponsard Hockey League – the community league northwest of Queen Mary Road in the Circle Road area of Côte-des-Neiges. The neighbourhood was somewhat tonier than Lower Snowdon, where we now lived. My dad's financial position had gone from daily crisis and disaster to the steady, if modest, income from driving a cab. My mom, able to move on from her job at the Medical Arts Pharmacy, used her background as a secretarial college graduate to find an office job at a vocational service organization near McGill on Sherbrooke. We lived in a duplex on West-bury near Van Horne, with three bedrooms and a small backyard. That duplex was a solid forty-five-minute to an hour walk from the outdoor rink and change house (with potbelly stove), where I played organized hockey. My abilities on the ice were limited. I was a defenceman, and my extra weight made the back and forth demanding. But you could never tell the coach that you were tired or needed a rest. It was much simpler to get a two-minute penalty and catch your breath in the box. If you needed more time, complaining to the referee about the penalty could win you five minutes, and swearing could net ten. Each level of the league replicated the six NHL teams. We all wanted to wear Maurice Richard's number 9 and be on the Canadiens team. I got to wear number 9, but my assigned team was the Chicago Blackhawks. Nonetheless, I played twice a week, my feet so frozen at the end of ninety minutes on an outdoor rink in Montreal's seriously cold winters that I had no feeling in my toes till well after my long walk home from the game. On occasion, one of my brothers or my dad would come and watch.

The Ponsard Hockey League, sponsored by Doug Harvey's Sporting Goods Store on Queen Mary, was the first outlet of my young life that was not shaped by religion, minority community expectations, or the sense of being an outsider. (Harvey had been a star defenceman for the Canadiens. His store later became Snyder's Sporting Goods, owned by Gerry Snyder, the deputy mayor of Montreal.) Families of all faiths and backgrounds had kids playing in that league. And though my family's modest circumstances meant that we bought our equipment second-hand in the back of the sports store, we weren't alone in so doing. I would never be scouted for the NHL – unlike my brother Seymour, who played so well in the industrial leagues that he was scouted by the New York Rangers. But if your team made it to the Cup Final, your last game was played on some forlorn Saturday afternoon in the Montreal Forum. The hockey banquet for all the players, volunteer coaches, and parents was usually held in the basement of St. Kevin's Roman Catholic Church, where a retired Canadiens old-timer would speak. Trophies and ribbons were awarded, and Chalet BBQ chicken was served. For an eleven-year-old from an immigrant community who was trying to understand the world in which he would need to manoeuvre, this experience couldn't have been better. Hockey was a magic portal to another world. (Many years later, when I attended early morning hockey games with my brother Brian and my nephew Scott, who played in a north Toronto amateur league, and saw the parents of all colours and nationalities lower their kids onto the ice and then gather together to drink the worst coffee in the world, I understood even more the seminal role of hockey in shaping a Canadian sense of belonging.)

▼

My parents rarely argued, and when they did it was about money, usually the necessity or suitability of some expenditure. I remember Dr. Goldberg coming to our home and giving me a shot to bring down my high fever. My dad shuffled nervously because the five dollars for the house call was simply not there. The doctor, who was equally embarrassed, said, "Morris, not to worry. We'll sort it out some other time." I recall my parents' embarrassment when the synagogue sent over several boxes of food for Passover because our circumstances had elicited some community help. I remember my mom's bitter anger when she couldn't afford a new dress for a family holiday gathering, humiliated at having to wear the one she'd worn many times before. Another time, I recall my father being told by his dad, my zaida, to leave the Passover table, go home, and change his recently bought cheap suit because, unlike his old suit, it did not have a union-made label in the lining.

"When you don't wear a union-made label, you turn your back on working people. Not at this table!" Zaida intoned.

For me, life was mostly a mix of school, hockey, food, friends, better-off relatives, and brothers who were beginning to date and work their way through high school. I asked Jewel, a bright and attractive school-mate from a well-off family, to be my date for the Grade 7 prom. She turned me down. A cab driver's son couldn't possibly make the cut. But I set that aside pretty quickly. The odd financial family calamity seemed to be over relatively swiftly. It never occurred to me that much could be done about it other than chug along day-by-day. That would soon change.

My father's last working years were spent as a cab driver – car number 99 – for the Veterans Taxi Company. By then, a combination of hard, frustrating jobs and the ravages of bad diet and heavy smoking, so often associated with the working poor, had taken its toll. He suffered from life-threatening nephritis, high blood pressure, and arteriosclerosis, a combined disease pathology that stood in the way of available therapies for each of his separate illnesses. He was deemed too old for renal dialysis, which, to be fair, in the 1960s was conducted on a machine that took up an entire room at the Royal Victoria Hospital on Pine Avenue. He was referred to the Pratt Diagnostic Clinic in Boston because of the complexity of his symptoms but came home with only a recommended hand cream for his perpetually dry skin. The clinic could do nothing substantial for him. It did, however, generate a huge bill that we had no hope of paying, a contributing factor to my father's declaration of bankruptcy.

As a cab driver, he worked eighteen hours a day and more. He began in 1961 with a rented taxi and then bought his own cab (a used 1958 Pontiac, along with a permit medallion), thanks to a loan from Uncle Hy, proprietor of the Quality Kosher Bakery in Rochester. By February 1965, my dad had made progress in paying back that loan. One Sunday morning, he brought home some brochures for a resort in Florida, where he hoped to book a week's vacation for my mom and himself. In almost three decades of marriage, this would have been the first holiday they had ever taken that did not involve mooching off relatives. But that night, my dad had a massive stroke, followed by two more strokes in the next twenty-four hours. He was gone by Tuesday morning.

He was only fifty-four. I was fourteen. His death hit me hard, as it would any young person, and its impact cannot be overstated. My mother's strength, frugality, and hard work enabled us to survive financially, though it was not easy. She inherited Dad's cab and medallion, which she rented out, and she had a reasonable secretarial income.

A lot of people came to the funeral home and to sit shiva in our apartment in Snowdon. They all had similar memories of my dad: very hard working, kind to others, but always on a tough uphill climb. Dad had had an infectious sense of humour. He spoke a rich combination of English, Yiddish, and Montreal street French. My strongest feeling after his death was not the fear of the unknown or angst about how we would manage. Mostly, I was angry: at the raw deal that life had handed him, with 24/7 menial jobs or no jobs at all. As a cab driver, he was out the door early in the morning; he came home for dinner but then headed out again, staying as late as the business demand required. On Sunday afternoons, he napped in front of golf or football on the TV. He paid rent on the cab and medallion, which were initially owned by the fleet, but finally managed to buy his own car and medallion, helped by Uncle Hy in Rochester. And just when he could finally breathe and plan ahead, a series of strokes had taken him.

It was all so sudden, with no chance for final reflection or a goodbye. I didn't know if he had died angry or at peace. What I did register was the futility of his hard life.

My anger was deep, and I had no idea what to do about it. Going to synagogue every morning for a year to recite prayers and Kaddish for the departed, also a tradition in our faith, was a bridge away from some of my rage, but it worked only for a while. My life was school, synagogue, and hockey, and none of these offered any real answers to my confusing emotions.

CHAPTER 4

A Special Assembly at School

▼

Optimism is the faith that
leads to achievement. Nothing can be done
without hope and confidence.

HELEN KELLER

▲

SPECIAL ASSEMBLIES AT MY primary school were few and far between. With a full secularized and religious curriculum to be covered, wasting time was not encouraged. The same was true for the adjacent high school that I was slated to attend, which housed students who were preparing for the McGill entrance exams and also studied a full Hebrew and half-day religious program. Elmer the Safety Elephant visited annually. A principal or a long-serving teacher might retire. There would be ceremonies for Grade 7 graduates and one for Grade 11 graduates. A fire drill or the assassination of a president (as in November 1963) could justify a gathering. Otherwise, there was work to be done, and studies always came first.

So when classes were told in mid-May 1962 – three years before my dad died – that an assembly for a special guest was planned for Friday, with all students from both schools expected to attend and all parents invited, rumours ran rampant.

I hoped the special guest would be a hockey player. Maybe the Rocket himself! Others thought it might be some visiting Israeli politician or perhaps Mr. Bronfman – that would be Sam Bronfman, the head of Seagram's and de facto leader of the Montreal Jewish community – to announce a new donation or further generous contribution.

On the day before the assembly, we learned that the guest would be Prime Minister John George Diefenbaker. The school was abuzz with excitement. A federal election was coming up in June, but our riding, Mount Royal, had been in safe Liberal hands forever. Alan Macnaughton, our MP and Speaker of the House of Commons, had held the seat since 1949. He had even beaten the Progressive Conservative candidate, popular mayor Reg Dawson of the town of Mount Royal, in the 1958 PC sweep, when Diefenbaker won the largest number of seats to that point in the history of Canadian elections. My dad, who was both a Liberal and busy driving a cab (you couldn't make money if you weren't out on the street), had no intention of attending the assembly. My mom had her office job downtown with a Jewish community vocational service, which was unlikely to grant an afternoon off for hearing a Progressive Conservative prime minister.

From my later vantage point, gained through years of helping to plan campaigns for party leaders, provincial premiers, and subsequent prime ministers, the logic of Diefenbaker's school visit is clear. Even in a hopeless riding, if you can fill a large, ready-made room with people who are warm and respectful, and can bring them a reasonable non-partisan message, everyone will agree that you've had a good outing. Besides, it always unnerves your opponents when, for any reason, you visit their safest seats. I knew none of this as a twelve-year-old, sitting in the auditorium. Mr. Diefenbaker was the prime minister – why on earth would he come here?

When the hour came and the PM arrived, his entourage was pretty small by today's standards. The Montreal police led the way, turning their motorcycles north off Victoria onto St. Kevin, where our school was situated. They were followed by two sedans, the first of which carried Diefenbaker and William Hamilton, the postmaster general of Canada and MP for Notre Dame de Grâce (elected in 1953). The other car held Egan Chambers, MP for Westmount, elected in the 1958 sweep, and Stan Shenkman, the young business leader and developer who was the Tory candidate in our riding. The Notre Dame de Grâce and Westmount ridings bordered our seat. A third car, carrying more police, brought up the rear.

When Diefenbaker emerged, he was greeted by the president of our school's board, Ben Beutel (my great-uncle by marriage, the prominent philanthropist who paid my school fees), as well as the principal and vice-principal. Our principal was a genial professor of Hebrew literature, Melech Magid. Our vice-principal was the efficient, compelling, and very much in charge Sadye Lewis, whose clipboard and whistle were the symbols of order and discipline. She also taught Grade 7 – firmly.

The gymnasium was packed. All classes from both the elementary and high school levels were there, as were all the teachers and the office staff. Worthies from the board and the community sat on the stage. Diefenbaker was introduced from the back of the hall to tumultuous applause. I found out much later that he always entered from the back of the hall; that's what he preferred.

His speech was not partisan in any way. He didn't seek votes or criticize the other parties. This was a school assembly, after all. But he did use the occasion to describe the Canada he believed in, listing some of the things he had done and outlining what he still needed to do to make the country the kind of home it should be for long-time citizens and new arrivals alike. He talked about raising pensions for older Canadians so that they might live with dignity. He talked about appointing the first woman to sit in a federal cabinet. This was Ellen Fairclough, an MP from Hamilton, who, as minister of citizenship and immigration, had brought in a points system to ensure that all applicants were assessed fairly, not on the basis of race, country of origin, or religion. He mentioned bringing in the Agricultural Rehabilitation and Development Act, whose purpose was to fight poverty in rural areas and keep Canadian farms competitive. He talked about selling wheat to China to fight hunger in that part of the world and to help Canadian farmers. He talked about his Roads to Resources Program and the TransCanada Highway initiative. But above all, he talked about the Canadian Bill of Rights that his government had presented to Parliament in 1960 and was now law.

His tone was explanatory but intense, his eyes flashing and his hands engaged. His stance at the podium, as he scanned all parts of the auditorium, conveyed a passion and sincerity that television could never properly capture. He spoke of his concern that people whose background was neither English nor French should never feel like second-class citizens. He told us that he could have used his mother's family name when he ran for office – Bannerman, a solid Scottish surname. He used Diefenbaker instead: "It's longer, it comes from my dad's Dutch-German origins, but it is as Canadian as any other name."

Diefenbaker explained that he had appointed the first Native Canadian (the term commonly used then) to the Senate and had also given Native people the right to vote. He spoke of how, when he practised law, he had defended Metis and other Native clients in Saskatchewan without charging them, because they deserved a fair deal, they deserved equality before the law, and he was distressed by people's poverty, their living conditions, and the injustices they faced. As I recall, he said, "In my Canada, we are all equal before the law. Discrimination because of your origin, your religion, is now against the law because of this Canadian Bill of Rights, which I have brought with me to present to your school."

His audience was made up of Holocaust survivors and their children, refugees from the poverty and bigotry of Eastern Europe, and the children of men who had fought for Canada in the Second World War. There were teachers who had immigrated from various parts of the world, seeking the economic opportunity and religious freedom that Canada offered. There were parents and grandparents who had been through the war and the Depression, folks who had gathered around the radio to listen to reports from the Second World War or from Korea and to reports of the combat in Suez.

At the time, I couldn't have known that though Diefenbaker would win the June election, his government wouldn't form a majority. What I did know was that this prime minister seemed to be consumed with making life better for people who faced tough times. He actually worried about poverty and exclusion. His passion, his chosen areas of focus, and the rhetorical impact of his words planted an idea in my mind, one that had never occurred to me before that Friday in May. It was not about food, or hockey, or my toy box, or religion. It was not about driving a taxi or working in an all-night drugstore. It was not about unemployment, or arrears in the rent, or hand-me-down clothes and second-hand skates. The idea was that one person who cared and fought for better things could truly improve people's lives. Life was not solely about your day-to-day ups and downs. It could be about helping others, getting beyond the mirror we all hold up to see our own reflections. It could be about reaching out and doing something for the broader community.

For someone from my background, that revolutionary idea contained more than encouragement. Its message came together quickly with deep-seated anxieties about poverty, economic insecurity, and fairness. Diefenbaker's words lit a pilot light inside of me. Life was not just about the next year of school or what I planned to do that summer. It was about finding a purpose above and beyond that, about the role even a kid from a lower-working-class family might be able to play.

Mr. Diefenbaker did not end his speech by asking for votes. He repeated the words from the speech he had delivered in Parliament on July 1, 1960, encouraging each of us to remember them always: "I am a Canadian, free to speak without fear, free to worship in my own way, free to stand for what I think right, free to oppose what I believe wrong, and free to choose those who shall govern my country. This heritage of freedom I pledge to uphold for myself and all mankind."

He then asked for our help, not for himself but for the country's future. I recall it this way: "The family table we call Canada is the finest table in the world. There is space and food enough for all. But I need your help to make sure that no one is denied a seat at that table because of the colour of their skin, the religion they believe in, or how well off they or their parents might be. Farmer, fisherman, factory worker, teacher, businessman, nurse, East or West, North or South, city or town. They are all part of the family, whether fifth generation or just recently arrived. We have to build a Canada that respects the rights of all and builds opportunity for each and every one! I need your help, everyone in this room, so that we can build that Canada together."

These words drew a line through the doubts and questions and hopes and fears of a twelve-year-old. It could not have been clearer. It was a line that led directly to politics. He had me with "I need your help."

How odd to think that a Prairie politician with a Baptist background and small-town roots could draw this line so clearly for a pre-pubescent Jewish kid from a hard-scrabble background, from a family of no consequence, with limited resources. For me, for better or worse, the notion of reaching out to help others, of standing up for people who were outside the mainstream, those excluded from the charmed circles of the establishment, became one and the same with supporting this Progressive Conservative prime minister and his party. I had no understanding of broader Conservative history or of how Diefenbaker's stance compared to that of the Liberals or others. What I did know, at that tender age, was that in my part of the world, the Liberals were the in-crowd, the folks on the make. In Montreal and throughout Quebec, the Liberal Party stood for inherited wealth.

That my dad had volunteered in a neighbouring riding for Liberal campaigns, that my grandfather had supported the CCF/NDP during his years in Canada, that the Montreal establishment and most of the "leaders" of the ethnic communities – Jews, Italians, Portuguese, Greeks – were also largely Liberal simply helped the equation form in my mind. Too many people were poor despite the apparent wealth of the country. Unemployment insurance did not really exist yet, and welfare and other minimalist supports were paltry and disconnected from real-life needs. In east-end Montreal, in Point St. Charles, poverty was not addressed in any practical way, except by the Salvation Army and other community organizations.

I still remember my excitement as I walked home after the Diefenbaker speech. There was work to be done, and this man, who understood human rights and fairness, needed my help. It was, to be sure, a fairly self-centred conclusion for a twelve-year-old student to reach.

At the dinner table that evening, the response to my enthusiasm was tepid, to say the least. My grandfather informed me that the Conservatives were the bosses' party. I respectfully reminded him that the bosses in the rag trade against whom he had organized a strike were Liberals, as were most business people in the Jewish community. My dad offered a quick "over my dead body" when I announced that I'd be volunteering my services for the election campaign of Stan Shenkman, our local PC candidate. My father's reaction, for understandable pre-teenage reasons, merely deepened my resolve.

Mom brought the intensity to an end by suggesting that I write to all the party leaders, seeking information on their respective platforms before I joined any effort. I agreed because, as the baby in the family, I tilted toward compromise and harmony. The next morning, I wrote the appropriate letters to Diefenbaker, Mike Pearson, Robert Thompson (Social Credit), and Tommy Douglas (NDP). But this was really only a gesture. Three leaders sent back mimeographed form letters enclosing a pamphlet. But Diefenbaker's office produced what appeared to be a personally signed note, encouraging me to join the Tories. The inclusion in the envelope of a few relevant Quebec-focused and human-rights-underlining speeches put a padlock on my decision. Diefenbaker and the Conservatives cared about average people, poor people, struggling people. They really did want to make Canada a better, more caring country. The others? Just going through the motions. I was a poor kid in a family of no consequence. The prime minister answered my letter!

As an aside, when in 1998 I was a candidate for the PC leadership, I decided to announce my health care policy at the Diefenbaker Centre, near his burial place at the University of Saskatchewan. After visiting the grave of Diefenbaker and his wife, Olive, and leaving a wreath, we went into the centre, where I made the announcement from behind his desk in a recreated Prime Minister's Office. After I finished, I mentioned that Diefenbaker had played a key role in the genesis of medicare. In 1961, shortly after Tommy Douglas put Saskatchewan's universal health insurance plan in place, Diefenbaker had asked Justice Emmett Hall to review its impact. By the time the Hall Report was completed, the Tories were no longer in power, so it was delivered to the new prime minister, Mike Pearson, and it became the basis for national medicare. I toured the centre, looked at books, memorabilia, and files. The curator then said that they had a special presentation for me. I was puzzled. They brought out a blown-up and mounted copy of my 1962 letter to Diefenbaker, as well as a copy of his response to me. Yes, I teared up.

To return to 1962, every setback in Stan Shenkman's campaign simply deepened my resolve. A decent and hard-working candidate, he ultimately garnered less than half of the Liberal's winning vote, thus losing his deposit. But a road had appeared to me, one of high-minded engagement for a better country, where everyone had the right to a fair shot.

The more the media came down on Diefenbaker (sometimes for good reason, as I learned over the years), the more I saw him as a victim of the establishment. When he clung to his minority in the June 1962 election, I identified with him even further. Without understanding all the nuances of Canada-US relations, I felt that the connivance between the White House and the Liberal Party to elect Mike Pearson in 1963 simply proved my point. Not only was Diefenbaker a "people's" guy, he was a nationalist, defending Canada against the nuclear weapons the Americans wanted to impose on us. During the lead-up to the 1963 election, a poll conducted by President John F. Kennedy's own Democratic Party pollster showed that a slim majority of Canadians favoured accepting nuclear warheads for our Bomarc anti-aircraft missiles. Pearson, who had long opposed nuclear weapons, now changed his stance, becoming prime minister as a result, another injustice to Diefenbaker. Over the decades, I would learn about Diefenbaker's imperfections, his excesses, and his inability to manage his own cabinet or Canada-US relations, but as I turned the corner toward high school, my support for him was rock-solid.

Three years later, when my dad died, I received condolence letters from teachers, rabbis, hockey coaches. Because of my volunteer work in the 1962 and 1963 federal election campaigns, I also received a brief, warm note from the Mount Royal riding president, expressing his sympathy. The note was written on PC stationery with an embossed PC flag logo – basically a Canadian maple leaf with blue rather than red borders. It reminded me of my "Diefenbaker moment" in 1962, and a small window opened to let in a clear ray of light. I felt a sense of duty related to that moment, and I pledged that I would assess every challenge by putting these questions to myself: Can this help make a difference to those outside the charmed circle? Will it matter? Can I be the one to make it matter in the larger battle against the cruel unfairness of the poverty that affects millions in Canada and worldwide? Is it worth doing? Would Mr. Diefenbaker have approved?

CHAPTER 5

Starting the Political Voyage

▼

Is there anyone so wise

as to learn from the experience of others?

VOLTAIRE

▲

THROUGHOUT HIGH SCHOOL, my interest in the kind of politics that bridged gaps would manifest in the courses I chose among my electives. I worked as editor of the school's monthly magazine, *Reflections*. I fought in support of a model parliament and finally got one going in our school. Although I did play hockey until Grade 9 and was a right tackle on the short-lived Herzliah High School football team, my interests centred on politics and history, as well as geography, French, English literature, and English composition – all subjects that would help me understand and contribute. I wanted to go to university in Ottawa. As the University of Ottawa offered courses in both official languages and had a superb history department, with Canadianist professors from both the Anglo and the Québécois traditions, it struck me as the very best choice.

In the summer before my thirteenth birthday, I signed up for a YMHA-sponsored youth hostelling program that took groups of young people with their bikes to explore three areas – Quebec City, Ottawa, and Cape Cod. This would be my first travel without my parents or brothers.

My visit to Quebec City in 1963 with others my age (we went by train, with our bikes stowed in the baggage car) was a serious eye-opener. In

Montreal that spring, several public facilities, military installations, and mailboxes had been bombed, allegedly by FLQ terrorists. In Quebec City, a statue of Wolfe on the Plains of Abraham had been unbolted and toppled. The FLQ was issuing manifestos that talked about both independence and poverty. Its historical analysis – that poverty generated unrest – was new to me. Was it true, or was it just a fabrication of extreme nationalists who would use any excuse? Later, of course, I learned about the mass poverty and economic despair that helped breed Marxist-Leninist insurgencies and coups, and even the Nazi putsch in the 1930s. But at the time, I had no understanding of the link between poverty, however abject or hopeless, and extremism or insurgencies. I had read about the Winnipeg General Strike of 1919, when mounted police charged a crowd of strikers, but I could not imagine that kind of violent outbreak in my lifetime. I remember asking myself, what could this possibly have to do with Canada? Our visits to the Assemblée Nationale, the boardwalk, and the Plains of Abraham, with its attendant museum, did not answer my question, but they provided some context.

Although our trip to Ottawa had a similar touristic frame, I came away enthralled. The changing of the guard, the Peace Tower, the Hall of Honour, and the old War Museum (on Sussex Drive) were all gripping. There were no proceedings to watch, but the House of Commons Chamber and the Senate Chamber reeked of history and immense gravitas. Visiting them was a totemic moment in my life. The concept of civility and order under the Crown as the best way for a democracy to sort out its differences filtered through all the sights and sounds and official events we attended.

Boston and Cape Cod were more about beaches and cookouts and staying at a youth hostel in Sandwich. The revolutionary historic points in the city struck me as overdone and a touch dramatic – as some Americans can be about their own history, to the exclusion of everyone else's. Yet the thought I had picked up in Quebec City re-emerged. When the perceived lack of fairness is widely felt, when the government of the day can be portrayed as uncaring, the seeds of real trouble are not hard to sow. My sense of some basic truths and consequences in politics and in life was definitely beginning to gel.

The forces at play in my world started to intensify with the hormonal and other imbalances of adolescence. On the one hand, the idea of

Canada as a peaceable kingdom, where civility and balance bred stability and freedom, was at centre ice. But a nagging angst, not unrelated to the precariousness of the near-poverty conditions in which my family lived, was ever present. A bailiff arriving to seize your dad's car and empty the house of furniture is not something that fades into distant memory. It stays solidly with you, like a dark spot at the edge of a slice of bread.

My father's sudden death the year after my bar mitzvah also affected me deeply. Being malnourished during his first nine years and not finishing even his primary education had subjected him to a gruelling and ill-rewarding work life. Chronic diseases, made worse by smoking, a bad diet, and the general pathologies associated with the working poor, played a major role in his early demise. My mom would live for another ten years, relatively robust and healthy, although smoking ended up taking her down with lung cancer at age fifty-seven. Her brothers and younger sister lived into their eighties, and as I write this, one of those brothers and the sister are heading into their mid- and late nineties. My family members all shared the same genes, but my parents' low income had clearly taken its toll. All of this kicked around in a corner of my grey matter.

My mother, a very together, kind, and smart lady, was now working as office manager at the B'nai Brith Youth Organization's Van Horne office, spending her professional time with teenaged members from the various B'nai Brith chapters in Montreal and beyond. BBG (B'nai Brith Girls) was her primary focus. It was like a toned-down Girl Guides, without the uniform and the Baden-Powell oath. But employing the values of family, leadership, respect for country, faith, and culture to help girls negotiate the joys and trials of adolescence was central. My mother dispensed advice and served as a listening post for hundreds of girls.

Every once in a while, I too would seek her advice, on the life choices, setbacks, and forks in the road that seem so dramatic at the mid-teen point in life. When the model parliament was being launched at school and taking up a lot of my time, Mom's advice was "moderation in all things. If the teachers think it's worthwhile, a good learning event, then work at it. But not at the cost of your studies." As my interest in politics grew (other kids had Beatles posters on their walls; I had posters of Diefenbaker and Daniel Johnson, the Union Nationale leader), she was practical but never discouraging. "Touie," she would say, "remember there are other ways to help the world besides politics – law, for example, medicine, dentistry, social work." I heard what she said, but I didn't really listen. The death of my dad had alerted me to how short life could be, and my increasing, if perhaps delusional, sense of duty told me that helping the most people possible was the ultimate measure of service and public engagement. In retrospect, an inspirational trinity made up of the bailiff, John Diefenbaker, and the Grim Reaper seems a little odd. But all three were driving forces, as was the memory of my favourite toy box, consumed in a poor man's empty furnace.

Of course, my early conviction was wrong. A doctor who finds a new treatment or a lawyer who protects human rights can affect millions more people than even the most effective, popular, and successful politician. I would understand this by my mid-thirties. But other events in my teens had me doubling down on the political route.

Joan Baez, the famous American folksinger, came to Montreal as part of a performing tour protesting the Vietnam War. Ted Lazarus, my colleague at the school magazine, and I decided that we would try to interview her. Her entourage said no press access – she was very angry at the relentless media pressure to discuss her painful breakup with Bob Dylan. But Ted suggested we approach our all-knowing headmaster, Arthur Candib, for advice on how we might get around that.

Mr. Candib was not only my headmaster. As well as being the key English literature teacher at Herzliah High School, he taught English at Sir George Williams University (now Concordia). His dad had been a non-kosher butcher in the Jewish part of town when my maternal grandfather ran Dankner's Bakery. Arthur Candib was the font of all wisdom, and he would teach a Shakespeare play by drawing a large diagram of a cow on the blackboard, then analyzing the play through comparing it to the parts of the cow. "This soliloquy is like the loin," he would say. "These characters are like the ribs. This event is like the rump." To this day, I look at a work of fiction or non-fiction and think where each piece would fit on the body of a cow. Not elegant, but helpful still.

"Teddy, Hughie, I read in *Time* that Miss Baez does not eat meat," Mr. Candib informed us. "Why not call up the Brown Derby and have them send a smoked fish platter to her suite at the Windsor Hotel, with a request for two student journalists to interview her for about an hour? Be respectful and courteous, and leave the school's phone number." We called the Brown Derby at 10:30 a.m., and it promised delivery by 12:30 to the hotel.

At 2:15, I left my Latin class to take a call in the office. It was a member of Joan Baez's staff, who said, "Mr. Segal, if you can be here by 3:00, you can have an hour. If you tell any other media, we will cancel your appointment."

"Yes, sir," I said. I borrowed cab fare from Mr. Candib, rustled up Ted from his math class, and grabbed the school's car-sized Webcore reel-to-reel tape recorder. We hopped in a taxi for downtown.

An aide waited in the lobby of the Windsor Hotel to take us up. I could smell the smoked salmon on her breath. "Thanks for the smoked fish platter," she said. "There was enough for all of us."

The room was a large suite, with a big sitting room, many other people, and a bed in the corner on which Baez sat with music sheets and a guitar. Ted and I were somewhere between curious, awestruck, and shy. But Joan Baez was elegant, courteous, and kind. Before we got started, she asked us about our magazine and our school.

Our questions to her were about the mood in the United States surrounding the controversy about the war, what she enjoyed most about touring, where else she was going in Canada, why she had decided to come to Montreal, and how much her music mattered in both the civil rights and anti-war movement.

Her answers were straightforward and direct. But one thing she said deeply impressed me: "The battle for civil rights and the battle against the war are really the same battle." I didn't understand the connection. She was gentle but clear in explaining: "Well, the draft sweeps up poorer young men who have no university deferments or parents well connected enough to work the system to protect their kids. A large percentage of these young men and their families are black or Hispanic. There aren't a lot of young men from well-off families being sent to Vietnam. Civil rights are about treating black and Hispanic Americans like all Americans, with the same rights to go to school, go to college, and get good jobs. Everybody should have the same choices as wealthy white American families and their kids. It is really the same fight."

I would never hear "We Shall Overcome," "Brothers in Arms," or "There But for Fortune," among the many songs she made famous, without reflecting on what she said that afternoon. After we had finished the interview, one of her staff gave Ted and me each a cassette of her music. We published the story in the school's mimeographed, stapled magazine a few days later.

Quite beyond the privilege of meeting and interviewing Baez, I had learned something profound: that poverty, human rights, and fairness were connected in far more intense ways than I had understood before.

In 1965, Lester Pearson won the federal election but not with the expected majority. Alleged Liberal Party corruption and other problems obscured much of his good work and achievements. Diefenbaker ran a folksy "he cared enough to come" campaign, visiting many small towns and rural communities by train.

In Mount Royal, I worked for the PC candidate Peter Wise, an accountant, who, along with the NDP candidate, the distinguished professor Charles Taylor, was beaten by newcomer Pierre Trudeau. He had joined the Liberals as a matter of convenience, after being invited to do so by Lester Pearson, along with Gérard Pelletier and Jean Marchand.

Alan Macnaughton, the Liberal MP since 1949, had been cleared out of the seat to make room for Trudeau. This sort of arrangement was not unique to the Liberals, but in an utterly safe seat – Canada's equivalent of a British "rotten borough" – it struck me as deeply symptomatic of how the political establishment moved the chess pieces exclusively in its own interest. That Pierre Trudeau came from inherited wealth (the Champlain oil fortune), had something of a dilettante reputation, and would take the riding's Jewish vote absolutely for granted was even more frustrating. To that point, he had leaned toward the NDP, or even farther left, and was deeply critical of Pearson's poll-driven 1963 conversion on the nuclear question. I saw the combined frames of his "to the manor born" background and his convenient Liberal candidacy as the kind of hollow opportunism that debased the currency of honest politics.

My loyalty to John Diefenbaker and his concern for the poor, for those outside the magic circle, for the immigrant, the farmer, and the pensioner, as well as the democratization of the party led by Dalton Camp, kept me glued to the Tories. I went to the 1967 leadership convention at Maple Leaf Gardens as a Diefenbaker supporter. "Youth for Dief," we were called. However, the winner of that close race was Robert L. Stanfield, ex-premier of Nova Scotia. I knew very little about him. He seemed decent and not given to the histrionics of his predecessor. But, after all, he had never visited my school, and Mr. Diefenbaker had.

CHAPTER 6

Clear Choices Emerge

▼

Liberty means responsibility.

That is why most men dread it.

GEORGE BERNARD SHAW

▲

GAINING ADMISSION TO THE University of Ottawa was one of the happiest days of my life. The news came in April 1968. Earning the McGill entrance certificate (the equivalent for private schools in Quebec of the provincial matriculation) meant that you entered a pre-university year in Ontario to start the usual three-year degree. This made up for Quebec high school ending at year 11 (as opposed to Grade 13 in Ontario).

My interest in the University of Ottawa sprang from three very different sources. First and foremost, it had superb historians, under whom I was eager to study. Cornelius Jaenen was an absolute master of the nuances of the Ancien Regime in Quebec, the role of the church, and the underlying sinews of French Canadian civilization, culture, and politics. Marcel Trudel was a distinguished expert, with a francophone and profoundly scholarly perspective on Quebec history. He was a founding partner behind the *Dictionary of Canadian Biography,* and his "Introduction to New France" remains a foundation piece for any serious study of Canadian history. I was also interested in Joe Levitt, who focused on Canadian political history, with a particular emphasis on "policy-driven history" and the role of individuals in shaping policy. His courses in US diplomatic history and

Canadian labour history would be important to my understanding of how the world worked. Levitt had written on Pearson's role in disarmament and Canada's nuclear weapons policy, covering the nuances of the 1963 election. And his analysis of the Winnipeg General Strike was magisterial.

My second reason for choosing the University of Ottawa was its location. It was only a few blocks from Parliament Hill – in close proximity to what my young mind saw as the centre of Canadian democracy.

The third thing that attracted me was the university's role as Ontario's bilingual post-secondary flagship. Unlike McGill, Concordia (then called Sir George Williams), or the Universities of Montreal and Laval, which in the 1960s and 1970s were either exclusively English speaking or exclusively French speaking, the University of Ottawa was defiantly and creatively bilingual. Not only were courses available in English and French, but anglophone students could take courses in French and write their papers and exams in English until their French fluency increased. Francophone students could do the same in English. Taking courses in the language that was not your mother tongue was encouraged, and there were also mandatory courses in French (at least two per year) in the early undergraduate years.

In 1965, the provincial government had purchased the University of Ottawa (the old Collège de Bytown) from the Oblate Order, thus bringing it into the publicly funded family of Ontario universities. This had been expanded and strengthened by William G. (Bill) Davis, minister of education and university affairs in the PC government headed by John Robarts. He had overseen the creation of Trent University in Peterborough and Brock University in Niagara, as well as the expansion of the Ontario Student Awards Program, which provided support beyond the Canada Student Loan Program. His policy commitment was that no qualified Ontario high school graduate would be denied access to post-secondary education because of funds, a stance that enabled poor and working-class kids and families to gain access to the economic mainstream. I would become deeply impressed with both Davis and his brand of conservatism during my years at university and beyond. By bringing in French-language and bilingual tertiary education, by expanding financial aid to low-income students, and by supporting the creation of the Colleges of Applied Arts and Technology, Davis was making inclusivity and equality of opportunity fundamental to the PC approach to higher education.

When, in later years, I learned that Bill Davis had stayed loyal to John Diefenbaker through elections when Diefenbaker's popularity was on the wane in Ontario, you can imagine what that meant for me. In fact, his entry into provincial politics had almost been stymied by the Diefenbaker government's decision to cancel the Avro Arrow jet fighter project, since there was an Avro plant in Davis's Peel riding. The project had been scrapped because, aside from the Soviets, who were Cold War enemies, and the Israelis, who allegedly wanted the aircraft donated to them, there were no takers for the Avro Arrow outside of Canada. Canada could not afford to manufacture the aircraft and also be its sole client. None of that mattered in a riding where thousands of folks were laid off just before the by-election of 1959, in which Davis was attempting to win a long-held Tory seat left vacant by the retirement of Premier Thomas Laird Kennedy, a former minister of agriculture. Davis was elected, but by a vastly reduced margin, one in the hundreds as opposed to the thousands.

At university, I joined the English Debating Society, travelling to Syracuse, Fredericton, and Toronto for inter-collegiate debating tournaments. One of my team members was François Gendron, a friend from Montreal. Our team won the 1969 Alistair B. McNair Trophy at the University of New Brunswick debating tournament, up against the Royal Military College, McGill, the University of Toronto, Harvard, New Brunswick, Dalhousie, Sir George Williams, Acadia, Manitoba, and Queen's. The interest in that event back on campus produced a group of fellow students who encouraged me to run for student government, known as SUUO/AGEUO, or the Student Union of the University of Ottawa/Association générale des étudiants de l'université d'Ottawa.

I was hesitant because I had arrived on campus just the September before, and my first year was academically heavy: compulsory philosophy, Russian, English literature, French composition, French literature, and French Canadian history. In addition to the debating society, I was also active with the Progressive Conservative Student Federation (PCSF) club on campus.

In the end, I decided to run for vice-president, a choice driven by several thoughts. The student governments, consistent with the Ontario Union of Students and the Canadian Union of Students, were quite hard left. On our campus and elsewhere, they crowed about the glories of Castro's regime, decried the evils of the military-industrial complex, and proclaimed the supremacy of the Marxist-Leninist view of life. Of course, they largely sided with Jane Fonda on Vietnam and criticized any American effort or initiative.

My grandfather's hard work for the International Ladies' Garment Workers' Union in Montreal was not always about getting the bosses to treat union members fairly. Often, it was about fighting the hardline communists who sought to break up union meetings. In fact, uncharacteristically for a strong backer of the CCF and the NDP, Zaida was mildly supportive of Presidents Johnson and Nixon on Vietnam. When world politics came up at the dinner table, his regular comment was that "stopping the communists anywhere we can is good for working men and women." I vividly remembered the 1962 Cuban Missile Crisis, the wailing of the air raid siren at Van Horne School across the park from our home, and how frightened my parents were about what might ultimately happen. My grandfather's view that this scourge of totalitarian communism was led by Nikita Khrushchev and his willing accomplice Fidel Castro was no doubt honed in part by his escape from Bolshevik Russia.

My college Progressive Conservatism was very much about the importance of institutions, as well as the need for a firm foreign policy to contain totalitarian communism and for domestic campus policies that addressed real student requirements and rights. That was one incentive for me to engage. Another was the fact that the SUUO/AGEUO election was to be hotly contested. The two candidates for president were Allan Rock, a first-year law student, and Mohammed Rajbally, a second-year nursing student. Rajbally had asked me to be his vice-presidential candidate, but this struck me as counterproductive because students voted separately for each position – president, vice-president, and four commissioners: finance, sports, services, and external relations.

Another incentive was my competition for the vice-presidency – J.T. Richard, Denis Monière, and William Babcock. Richard was the son of the Liberal MP for Ottawa Vanier (formally Ottawa East), the riding in which the university was situated. A member of the campus Liberal establishment, he was a popular and likeable personality who ran with the sons and daughters of high-ranking judges, civil servants, military figures, and others. Students of less exalted birth called them the "Chateau Clique." Denis Monière, a *sciences sociales* student, was an appealing candidate, but he was quite hard left, as was generally the case with students and professors in his department. William Babcock was a celebrated anglophone student in English lit and a bit of a personality on the cultural scene. That made two anglophones (Richard and Babcock) up against one francophone. On a campus that was split pretty well fifty-fifty between anglophones and francophones, Denis would have an undeniable edge.

That being said, I had noticed a few defining things about our student body. The catchment function for post-secondary francophone education meant that many of our students came from small-town New Brunswick, Saskatchewan, Quebec, and northern and eastern Ontario. On the whole, they weren't as well off as the students down the Rideau Canal at Carleton or back at McGill or even the University of Montreal. And unlike at the University of Montreal, very few had gone through tony *collèges classiques* such as Collège Jean-de-Brébeuf, favoured by the higher-end Québécois families (and from which Pierre Trudeau had graduated). Instead, they came largely from *écoles secondaires* of the French-Catholic variety in Hearst, Cornwall, Sudbury, Timmins, Hull, Bathurst, and Hawkesbury, and they were a very working-class mix. Like me, they depended on bursaries and loans from one province or another and on the Canada Student Loan Program. My instinct was that a student government should focus on genuine services and advocacy that would assist lower-income students to negotiate their way through academia. Fussing with global Marxist struggles (such as being part of the multi-campus anti-Vietnam trend) should take a back seat.

I knew Allan Rock only in passing. He seemed engaged, eloquent, and down to earth. He had been a Paul Hellyer Liberal in the 1968 leadership convention that chose Pierre Trudeau, which in my view made him less of the Chateau Clique establishment than many others. I would see that Rock also had an infectious sense of humour and a healthy dose of idealism about fairness, the law, and the way the university pie should be split up. Our campaigns, his for president and mine for vice-president, were not hostile to each other.

My campaign committee soon formed up. Some of its members came from the debating society or the PCSF, including my friend John Hoyles from Val D'Or, whom I had met in English class during pre-university year, and Michelle Tremblay, a linguistics student I had met in French language lab. Sharon Ellerton, a friend from pre-university who came from Hull (now Gatineau) was also engaged. We were a small but happy crew.

Sabatino (Sam) Cardarelli, right defensive tackle for the famed Gee-Gees football club, and Ron McLaughlin, heavily involved in the Commerce Students' Association, also put their shoulders to the wheel. Ian Green, a geography major who worked at the *Fulcrum* (the English-language student paper), helped with the concept and tenor of my campaign message. Later, he became a roommate.

Somehow, we built a coalition of common law students, arts and history majors, the football team, and students from nursing and domestic sciences around the simple idea that student government should be about services on campus and students having more formal input. We proposed instituting course evaluation, in which students would get a say on the relevance and value of their courses; reducing the four-year compulsory philosophy requirement for the undergraduate degree; improving facilities; and enhancing financial help for students at risk. To everyone's surprise, I was elected vice-president in the April 1969 campus-wide contest. Allan Rock was elected president by a larger plurality than I was elected vice-president.

As I would soon discover, though student government had many back stops provided by the university administration, it was also a useful platform for understanding the general dynamics of government in Canada.

Each faculty (arts, commerce, nursing, social science, common law, civil law, graduate studies, medicine, engineering, and theology, called *sciences religieuses*) elected its own executive, which had seats on the Grand Council of the Student Union. Council meetings were bilingual. Many of our discussions and negotiations ran afoul of unavoidable differences in opinion between commerce and common law (to the right and federalist) and social science and civil law (to the left and usually sovereigntist in the Quebec context). The council was a miniature but accurate reflection of how, in some measure, Canada itself had been cobbled together yet continued to work.

The university rector, with whom the council had to work, was Father Roger Guindon, whose family had roots in Cornwall and small-town Quebec. He was a senior member of the Oblate Order, held a doctorate in statistics, and was a warrior in the battle for a bilingual university that knit together Canadians from all walks of life – the Anglo minority in Quebec, Franco minorities across Canada, and the Quebec French-speaking majority – into a coherent whole. It would be replete with differences but engaged through goodwill and understanding in building something greater than the sum of its parts.

Father Guindon began most of his speeches with a statistical reflection on who was who on campus and in Canada. He was true to his discipline in that way. His decency, sense of humour, and integrity were a huge part of his leadership. He was ably backed up by a vice-rector (administration), Allan Gillmore, who had been the first executive director of the Wascana Centre Authority, a major regional urban and parks development body in Regina. Gillmore's roots were in the remarkably frugal administrative practices of the NDP Prairie tradition, symbolized by premiers such as Tommy Douglas and Allan Blakeney (and, later, Roy Romanow).

Classically, as student union vice-president, I would visit the vice-rector's office to inquire about more funding for programs on campus, more financial help for students in need and more investment in health care and athletic programs for students. Every discussion would begin with Gillmore pulling down a roll-out banner from the blackboard frame. It featured two pie charts, one showing the university's expenditures and one showing its revenues. At that time, student fees produced minimal direct revenue. Indeed, the basic income unit grants from the Province (calculated per student, weighted by the complexity and level of the program he or she was taking) counted for more than the income from student fees. Special research grants and University Affairs Construction Program grants for projects approved by the Province were also a major source of revenue, as were grants for bilingualism from both Ottawa and Queen's Park. The university, which had become part of the publicly funded system only in 1965, had no private endowments to speak of. Academic salaries occupied the biggest slice of the expenditures pie chart, followed by administrative wages and the usual breakdown of utility and maintenance costs. I routinely argued that the amount spent on student services was too small. The response was courteous and considered, leaving some room for negotiating, but a rhetorical question always hung in the air – "Where should we cut to provide more for student services?" During these meetings, I learned about core realities – about progress by inches, trade-offs, and incremental change. I also came to understand that the primary motive of all bureaucrats is to protect their own jobs – a thought that frequently resurfaced when I later reflected on welfare reform.

When Allan Rock and I began our term of office in the spring of 1969, we inherited a deficit of about $6,000 from the previous SUUO/AGEUO administration. Coincidentally, our student union paid an annual fee of a dollar per student, or about $6,000, to retain its membership in the Ontario Union of Students (OUS). The OUS was becoming more and more self-reverential and radicalized, but Allan and I had both campaigned for a student union that would spend the fees it collected on services and benefits for students on our own campus. Allan dispatched me to an OUS meeting in Toronto to see if anything could be mitigated in favour of more services for students related to things such as group insurance, reduced group travel costs, or summer work programs. I found no interest in the reorientation of fees collected at the province-wide level. "Our service is that of defending student values and the values of global justice and social revolution worldwide," said one of the hard-left poohbahs at a meeting I attended. God spare me!

Allan and I agreed that the central value of a province-wide student union should be service to its members, and he was enthusiastic about the recommendation that we withdraw from the OUS. We made that proposal to the Executive Committee of the SUUO/AGEUO at its next grand council meeting. The vote was close, and the OUS proponents argued eloquently for the need to support the great ideological battle, including opposition to the Vietnam War. But they were out-voted, and our proposal was approved. Our student union withdrew from the OUS, and the $6,000 we saved erased our deficit.

The OUS subsequently became more radicalized, cutting off all formal consultation with the Ontario government and specifically the Ministry of University Affairs, Minister Bill Davis, and Deputy Minister Ed Stewart. As a result, the Ontario Student Awards Advisory Committee, made up of university administrators, Faculty Association reps, provincial public servants, members of the Council of College Regents, and student reps, no longer had any university student representation. The committee needed students for both balance and legitimacy.

Minister Davis wrote to Allan Rock and invited him to join the committee. Allan, however, was engaged with the rigours of law school and with re-orienting the programs and mission of the student union. He was also more interested in federal politics than in provincial, but he agreed that our student union should join the advisory committee. "Hugh," he said to me, "you're the vice-president. I'm delegating you to represent this student body."

Having some personal experience with being a starving student, utterly dependent on the largesse of the Bourse Étudiant Québec, as well as on summer and part-time work to pay my way through university (my mom, though a self-sustaining widow, was in no position to contribute), I saw joining the committee as a way of helping not only University of Ottawa students but needy students right across Ontario. And, because I received needs-based financial assistance from another province, I would not be in any conflict of interest. I attended my first advisory committee meeting at the Lord Simcoe Hotel in downtown Toronto in June 1969.

When you are nineteen, from a low-end working-class home in another province, and you see first-hand how what was then Canada's wealthiest province manages a critical issue of financial accessibility and equality of opportunity – well, it couldn't have taught me a better lesson. And parts of the process would have a deep impact on my view of how government actually worked.

Also at the committee meetings were Don Bethune, manager of the Ontario Student Awards Program (OSAP), and Alan Gordon, the assistant deputy minister. Agenda items covered how OSAP was performing, the amount of assistance afforded in total and per applicant, the economic circumstances of applicants and recipients, and the percentages of admissions at universities and colleges of students receiving financial aid. Debates centred on OSAP's relationship with the federally sponsored Canada Student Loan Program, the nature of the payback rules, and how the program rules might be improved or changed. The plan was that once a year Minister Davis would attend for lunch, taking questions and hearing comments from committee members.

Every few meetings, the deputy minister of colleges and universities, Ed Stewart, who had risen through the ranks from teacher and principal at Windsor's Kennedy Collegiate, would join us to talk about the broader picture of the post-secondary system in the province. We spoke about the rapidly expanding system of Colleges of Applied Arts and Technology, created under Davis's leadership and reflecting his strong view that all high school graduates had the right to post-secondary education. We also discussed the new universities, Brock and Trent, the mix between undergraduate and graduate education populations, the challenges of recruiting faculty, and the construction dollars committed to province-wide university and college expansion – in other words, the entire picture. We also referred to the importance of TVOntario, the Ontario Science Centre, and the University of Toronto's Ontario Institute for Studies in Education in taking education to a broader community. All three were founded by Davis.

You couldn't listen to either Davis or Stewart without being impressed by their commitment to post-secondary education as a liberating force, as a path out of poverty, as a bridge into the economic mainstream for minorities and immigrants, and as a bulwark that was fundamental to Ontario's core values, along with agriculture, industry, the rule of law, and human rights. That was the good part.

The bad part was that when Davis and Stewart weren't present, any substantial proposal for change – such as treating poor students as citizens rather than supplicants for rules-based temporary aid – would be stopped dead by bureaucrats and labelled as "forwarded for future study."

At one point, the Ontario Confederation of University Faculty Associations (OCUFA), which was represented on the committee by the erudite and engaging professor Chuck Hanly, proposed an alternative to OSAP. The OSAP program had many flaws – it was rules-based, pettifogging, and deeply bureaucratic. Applicants had to prove their poverty, report any and all income, and until absent from their parental home for a two-year period, divulge their parents' income as well. This produced a series of sliding scales that generated formulaic criteria for the annual eligibility between loan and grant. Like welfare, the program discouraged students from taking on paid employment, since it simply reduced their eligibility for assistance. The formula also had a very crude way of measuring the income of parents who, for any number of reasons, might not be financially capable of sending a child to university but who, on paper, had a high enough income to preclude the student from applying for assistance.

As noted, and as is the case with welfare in all Canadian provinces, OSAP applicants had to prove poverty to be eligible. But when it was suggested that people on welfare might also receive OSAP assistance, the bureaucrats quickly scuttled any notion of change.

OCUFA proposed a program called CORSAP – the Contingent Repayment Student Assistance Program. It had several governing premises:

- The distinction between student aid and direct per-student grants to universities from the Province would be surrendered.
- The full per-student cost of running the university would become the annual fees owing by the student.
- The Province would pay the tuition fees of students whose earnings were below a certain threshold.
- After a student graduated and found employment, the repayment of his or her student loans would be automatic as a percentage of the annual taxes paid by every citizen.
- Those doing well economically in the workforce would pay more in taxes, therefore more in student loan repayment.
- A progressive tax system would fully finance university education, and tuition fees could go up to reflect its unsubsidized actual costs.
- Annual provincial decisions regarding how much money would flow to universities and how much tuition fees could be increased would be replaced by a market-based system in which some universities could charge more in tuition and low-income students would be backstopped by the progressive tax system.

Aspects of CORSAP were no doubt radical, but bureaucratic rejection of the proposal was swift and comprehensive. Bureaucrats would lose the ability to decide annually who received what, institution by institution, formula by formula. The "cap in hand" relationship between universities and the Ministry of University Affairs would be diluted. Institutions with better reputations and higher standards would be able to charge more. University administrators disliked CORSAP because it put the university into a client-like relationship with students, in which students might matter more and have some client-driven choices. The proposal was dead in its tracks, even though many students were supportive. I was not the only member of the OSAP advisory committee who saw its merits. The applied colleges' representative, also a student, and representatives from the business community were in favour of CORSAP.

As I watched this idea die, despite inspired advocacy from Chuck Hanly, I rediscovered something I had not fully understood. Even the best of governments, led by the best of people and staffed by the finest of public-spirited civil servants, will see self-preservation as their primary mission.

Surrendering the power to make annual budgetary decisions or to use so-called ministerial or bureaucratic discretion meant reducing government's importance and essential role in the day-to-day – not a wise career-building strategy for any public servant. Learning this at an early age (I was between nineteen and twenty-one when I served on this committee) set me on a path of healthy skepticism about programs that are minutely micromanaged by government, however well intentioned the program or well meaning the civil servants involved.

My new realization dovetailed directly with the battles I undertook as vice-president back on campus, encouraged by both President Allan Rock and members of the grand council. One of our first targets was the requirement that undergraduates must take a philosophy course every year. We wanted students to have more elective choices, not remain tied to a centuries-old view of what was essential to education. Moreover, Thomist philosophy (from the thirteenth-century saint Thomas Aquinas) took up the first two years in the compulsory curriculum structure, meaning it was that long before one might study Hobbes or Locke or, heaven forbid, Burke, Bentham, Marx, or Sartre.

At a university that had been run by the Oblates from 1848 to 1965, getting the philosophy requirement changed was an uphill battle. So was the struggle to achieve a course evaluation process, whereby students could pass judgment on the content, quality of teaching, and dynamic of their courses, which would benefit future students and force professors to face a bit of accountability. Both engagements meant long negotiations with Father Guindon, Dr. Maurice Chagnon, who was the vice-rector (academic), and others. I reported back to the student government executive meetings and the grand council. In the end, student course evaluation was phased in, and the compulsory philosophy requirement was reduced to two years.

Ironically, I quite liked philosophy as a subject. I found it a serious test of my reasoning and deductive capacities, and I enjoyed discovering the clear and more nuanced differences between philosophers of the same era. Further study revealed what the nuances meant and why they were significant. Philosophy taught me to appreciate the various takes on our relationship with the world. I learned to value the empire of ideas and to perceive its impact on daily life, as well as on the understanding of what is real, what is spiritual, and why both matter.

I also got on well with, and truly liked, the Oblate priests. As involved, competent scholars and lecturers, they were genial, engaging, and bright. In fact, through my courses in theology, which was my minor concentration, the differing articles of comparative religious doctrine blended well with my interest in Canada's history, both our European settler histories and the larger history of European civilization as played out in Canada between Protestants, Catholics, and others. Sadly, back in the 1960s and 1970s, there was almost no reference to Indigenous peoples, whose civilizations long predated the arrival of Europeans.

As it turned out, I would do well enough in religious science to be invited by the head of the department to consider graduate work in that discipline. I think the subject suited me because, unlike many of my young Catholic fellow students, I did not see core principles of faith, such as original sin, the virgin birth, papal infallibility, or transubstantiation, as doctrines to be contested or questioned. For twelve years, my own religious education had been deeply entrenched in the core tenets of the Jewish faith: the Abrahamic covenant made by God regarding the Promised Land, the incontestability that the hand of God had written the Ten Commandments, the rigours of the Sabbath, and the kosher dietary laws. Early on in high school, I had determined that articles of faith and iron-clad laws from the past, or those based on specific, quite literal interpretations of the Old Testament, were not about logic. They were about discipline, about maintaining one's faith as separate from others. For that reason, it seemed foolish to contest them, whatever one's private views.

So, at university, I learned the principles of various faiths and of the catechism without personal anxiety. By contrast, many students were caught up in the atmospherics and histrionics of a pervasive *contestateur* mindset, which applied as much to the Vietnam War as to the growing use of pot on campus. The general view of my social science buddies was that all government was corrupt. I did not believe that all established wisdom, rules, and structures, or the broad social order itself, were flawed simply because they had existed for decades or centuries. I was, in that sense, a conservative. I thought the problem with the Vietnam War was that it was not being prosecuted effectively, not that it was intrinsically evil. I did believe that order and freedom were inextricably interdependent. Even in Joe Levitt's fascinating classes about the Winnipeg General Strike, I sided with Prime Minister Robert Borden and Minister Arthur

Meighen. Disorder was no framework within which to fairly sort out problems.

My decision not to pursue graduate studies in religious science was grounded in economic realities – once I had taken my degree, I needed to make a living to pay back my student loans. Any further study would have to satisfy my intellectual curiosity and give me job skills at the same time. Had that not been the case, continuing my studies in religion or philosophy might well have been on my list.

By the time I was elected president of the student union in the spring of 1970, I was well focused on making constructive progress while maintaining open, engaged relationships with my interlocutors, however I might disagree with their purposes or biases. My negotiations with the Oblates had taught me the rules of engagement – that fairness and respect for the other side meant refraining from questioning its motivation, even while challenging its judgment. Not all change was good; not all resistance to change was bad. The years to come would give me a serious new understanding of genuine injustice. Learning not to roll over in the face of it while remaining civil was the beginning of wisdom for a young Tory.

CHAPTER 7

Policy Linkages and a New Idea

▼

The difficulty is not so much in developing

new ideas, but in escaping from old ones.

JOHN MAYNARD KEYNES

▲

IT SOMETIMES HAPPENS that events and people converge to have a permanent effect on one's view of the world. That was certainly true for me during my years at the University of Ottawa, when bigger events connected with my daily life in ways that were fundamental to who I became and the central political cause I would promote. I had, after all, campaigned on a student bill of rights, to ensure some fairness in the relationship between students and the administration and to underline that rights were beyond any facile absorption with right or left.

In 1967, a year before I began my university studies, a civil war flared up between Nigeria and the breakaway state of Biafra. During the next three years, a million people would die in a conflict that had both political and religious overtones. I had heard nothing about the Biafra situation before registering at the University of Ottawa and had no awareness of its larger implications.

In early October 1968, two Canadian members of Parliament, Andrew Brewin, a New Democrat from Toronto, and David MacDonald, a Progressive Conservative from Prince Edward Island, visited Biafra to look into allegations of war crimes and other horrific excesses by the Nigerian

Armed Forces. Upon their return, they reported to the House of Commons that they had encountered evidence of mass starvation. As a member of the Commonwealth, Nigeria was a signatory to principles about the rule of law, democracy, and human rights that were at the very core of the Commonwealth mission and purpose. The British government sided with Nigeria, whereas Christian church groups and missionaries aligned with the Biafran position, Biafra being largely Christian. In August 1968, when questioned in Parliament about the war, Prime Minister Trudeau had offered a nonchalant and dismissive, "Where's Biafra?" Whether intentionally or not, his reply conveyed the sort of arrogance and condescension that would not serve his career or reputation particularly well. By September, Trudeau had indicated firmly that working with any entity other than the Nigerian government was not on. Biafra was in no way like Quebec, and the Nigerian government was brutal in ways that a Canadian government would never countenance. Nonetheless, the Trudeau government's bias toward the central government in the Nigerian federation was clear and oppressive.

Trudeau's throwaway line was the first noticeable blemish on his sun king image – not a bad thing, from my partisan perspective. With PC leader Robert Stanfield encouraging a robust Canadian position at the United Nations in support of humanitarian aid for Biafra, and Foreign Minister Mitchell Sharp torn between his own concerned instincts and British pressure to stay out of it, Ottawa seemed caught in its own sandal straps. In response to MacDonald and Brewin's pressure for humanitarian assistance, the United Kingdom pushed Ottawa not to send aid directly to Biafra via Canadian Armed Forces Hercules aircraft, but only through Lagos, because that city housed the Nigerian government. In all of this, sensitivities related to Quebec were not irrelevant in the Quebec-centric federal cabinet.

Early in 1969, MacDonald and Brewin were invited to visit the University of Ottawa as part of the Faculty of Arts speakers' series, for which I was one of many volunteer organizers. Andy Brewin had a scheduling conflict, so David MacDonald came on his own. His inherent decency and his articulate and clearly understandable account of what he had found electrified his listeners. The fact that MacDonald had worked across party lines, setting aside partisanship to put humanitarian interest first, was also quite rare back then.

MacDonald had been elected in 1965 and so was in his second term representing the PEI riding of Egmont, which encompassed Summerside and all points west, including Tignish at the far end of the island. Before entering politics, he had come to prominence as a United Church minister in Alberton, working with a Catholic priest, Father Gerry Steele, to tackle issues of alcoholism, family violence, and poverty. These were all connected. This kind of ecumenical cooperation was radical in mid-1960s Prince Edward Island, as a glance at its electoral system reveals. For many decades, every island riding had elected two provincial members, one for the Executive Council (formerly the upper house) and one for the legislature (formerly the lower house). But their separation was a creative fiction because they all sat as equals in the provincial Legislative Assembly. However, the dual-member system enabled each political party to run a Catholic candidate against the other party's Catholic candidate. Ditto with each party's Protestant candidate. Protestants and Catholics never ran against each other. Historically, the Catholic-Protestant divide was not without its unpleasantness, so a Protestant minister and a Catholic priest working on a joint community-focused initiative was without precedent.

In the 1965 federal election, when Prime Minister Pearson tried and failed to win a majority, seats like Egmont, in which David MacDonald beat long-time Liberal MP and postmaster general J. Watson MacNaught, made all the difference. MacDonald had survived the Liberal sweep of 1968 in large part because Nova Scotia, Prince Edward Island, and Newfoundland remained loyal to Robert Stanfield, the former premier of Nova Scotia. MacDonald was also popular as a community-engaged pastor who married, baptized, and buried his constituents, along with providing counsel and mediation in many rural areas when the local minister took a summer break. David was a key member of the progressive Red Tory left of the PC Party and caucus. His biases were communitarian, and he was deeply non-partisan on issues of public welfare, inclusion, and fairness. He was a very different kind of PC MP.

I recall David MacDonald's Biafra speech at the University of Ottawa as if it were yesterday. He talked about what poverty looked like in Africa and the extent to which aspects of the civil war were about resource revenues, jobs, and who was in charge of what. The Igbo people, who were the majority in Biafra, reasonably wanted their share of oil royalties to deal with economic deprivation in their own region; the federal government in Lagos refused. The fact that the Igbos were largely Christian, whereas Nigeria was Muslim, did not help.

My courses in Canadian, European, and American diplomatic history had referenced the effects of the Depression on economic outcomes in Europe, Canada, and elsewhere. But the deployment of violence between groups warring over resources had never been as directly portrayed to me as in MacDonald's first-person account. Of course, history is littered with events that would yield a similar point upon even the most cursory study, but I had never heard a contemporary struggle described in such stark, real-world terms. A new canal opened in my brain, and I immediately signed up to work as a volunteer in MacDonald's Ottawa office. It was the start of a professional, working, and learning friendship that would go on for decades.

In the spring of 1969, as a direct result of my volunteer work with David MacDonald and my active membership in the Progressive Conservative Student Federation at the university, some of the more "progressive" Progressive Conservatives invited me to help organize a policy retreat at an Oblate summer camp at Little Whitefish Lake, Quebec. The retreat was set up to give unofficial consideration to where the party should head as we prepared for the coming election in 1972. Robert Stanfield had won a respectable seventy-five seats in the 1968 election. But the Trudeau government was still very popular. There were many divergent positions as to what road the Tory party should take for the future. At least five views had already been proposed by caucus members, ranging from the urban to the rural, from the centrist to the hard right, from the pro-business and small-government frame to the steady-as-she-goes and smart smaller-government versus large-government bias. Robert Stanfield, though definitely of the centrist-pragmatic school, tilted toward the more humane, progressive side of the ledger, as opposed to the more right-wing, anti-government view espoused by Albertans such as Stan Schumacher and Jack Horner.

The small Quebec Tory caucus elected in 1968 was more nationalist than the Liberals, who had been elected in large numbers in that province. These Quebec Tories were not necessarily in support of "French Power," with which the Trudeau government was associated, but they favoured provincial rights, an important tenet of the centre-right in

Quebec politics from Maurice Duplessis and the Union Nationale to the present. The Union Nationale was the Tory party's natural base in many parts of Quebec, there being no provincial Progressive Conservative Party per se. Ironically, it had been formed during the Depression through the amalgamation of nationalist conservatives and progressive liberals who favoured the nationalization of Quebec's hydro-electric companies to preserve popular economic rights against the power of private monopolies. In this respect, it was very similar to the Ontario Conservatives, who created Ontario Hydro in 1906. When Robert Stanfield was premier, he had founded Nova Scotia Power, a Crown corporation, for many of the same reasons. "What are the public benefits of a power company that is private but also a monopoly?" the Harvard-educated lawyer, scion of a large manufacturing company, and former member of the wartime price board was known to ask. Many of today's privatizing Tories are undoubtedly unaware of the history that Conservative forces played in replacing private monopolies with publicly owned and administered corporations.

Although the Little Whitefish retreat was not an official meeting (as in sponsored by party headquarters or financed by the party), David MacDonald, its key organizer, had spoken with Stanfield. The PC leader was pleased that the retreat was under way and looked forward to its recommendations. Several party stalwarts attended it. These included party president Frank Moores, an MP from Newfoundland, and Nate Nurgitz of Manitoba, who was party vice-president for the West. Flora MacDonald, then secretary of the Political Science Department at Queen's University, attended too. A long-time supporter of Stanfield, she had been fired by John Diefenbaker because she was loyal to party president Dalton Camp. Roy McMurtry, a young lawyer from Toronto, participated, as did Rudy Dallenbach, a specialist in rural development from Macdonald College at McGill. They were joined by about twenty-five policy-focused conservatives from across the country who essentially wanted the next campaign to be about a better life for Canadians, not just winning the election.

Flora MacDonald took the lead on the issue of urban policy. She spoke, not of macro-policy solutions for the cities, but rather of policies connected to quality of life issues – poverty, housing, health, child care. They would improve prospects in communities, narrow the gap between rich and poor, and be grounded in a populist approach that was genuine and fact-based and that spoke to compassion and smart government. With some fresh ideas about community-based services, that theme meant more local flexibility, more community engagement, more of a role for MPs in local policy and service design. Rudy Dallenbach, who had an international development history as both a scholar and a rural develop-ment officer, argued for reforming and democratizing the Agricultural and Rural Development Agency. He pointed out that much could be learned from best practices elsewhere in the world, such as Western Europe, Israel, and the more progressive parts of Africa. The underlying theme was clear: politics that was not about fairness, government that was not about the most sensitive and effective way of promoting fair-ness, would ultimately be irrelevant. The old top-down, whatever-it-takes-to-win approach was not viable in a modern Canadian political party. If we wanted to be back in contention, we needed to be about community and local engagement.

Throughout the discussions about fairness and local sensitivity, eco-nomic fairness was central. Farmers needed important supports such as supply management for dairy and poultry, the Crown rate to keep grain shipping costs reasonable, and government-subsidized crop insurance. If the PC Party wanted to be relevant in cities, it also needed to improve the quality of life in urban settings, which included minimum living and environmental standards. By the time of this gathering, the Nixon White House had already begun shaping a family benefits guarantee to address the challenge of inner-city poverty. People in Canadian conservative cir-cles had taken notice and were reflecting on what all that meant.

Our group at Little Whitefish Lake agreed that we fell within the British tradition of political "ginger groups." Loyal to the larger party, a ginger group works within it to achieve constructive policy change and innovation. In fact, we all agreed that failing to work for better party poli-cies would be disloyal and that the ginger group strategy was not the exclusive preserve of left-wing parties. We also decided that we would share the results of our discussions, not only with the leader's office but also with those who attended the PC Party's Priorities for Canada Conference, slated to be held in Niagara Falls that autumn. We would carry our wisdom, such as it was, to the larger and official party confer-ence. David MacDonald shouldered part of that task.

Participating as an equal at Little Whitefish Lake, though young, inexperienced, and by far the most junior party member in the room, gave me a profound sense of the PC Party as an open place, far less establishment-focused and tethered than the federal Liberal Party. Here I was, the son of a cab driver and the grandson of dirt-poor refugees from Communist Russia, invited to attend and participate with others. A follow-up meeting at Macdonald College, McGill's agricultural school, co-chaired by Rudy Dallenbach, was a further demonstration of the urbane, community-focused, localist, and progressive branch of conservatism in Canada. The party as I experienced it was not defined by left or right, but by communitarian views of fairness and opportunity and the appropriate balance between freedom and order, profit and fairness, and genuine equality of opportunity.

The Niagara conference that October was a large affair, quite over-whelming to a delegate from the PC student federation at the University of Ottawa. It also demonstrated the irony that though a political party is often the incubator for new people and ideas, its internal strains and pressures can dilute genuine creativity and innovative thinking. This is particularly true of parties that aspire to be pan-national in stance and appeal, especially when they are in Opposition.

Shortly before the conference, the Tory research office brought out a paper on guaranteed annual income (GAI), which was prepared by Keith Banting, a young executive assistant to the director. Stanfield had spoken encouragingly about its recommendations – that essentially the welfare system should be totally reformed and that open consideration should be given to a GAI.

Some months earlier, President Richard Nixon had strongly supported the idea of a GAI and had touted it as part of his Family Benefits Plan, which aimed at keeping inner-city families together. Other advocates included economist Milton Friedman, economist and philosopher Friedrich Hayek, and even Democratic Party presidential hopeful George McGovern. Doing away with income-tested and micromanaged programs appealed to right-wing Conservatives because it reduced bureaucratic growth, but it also appealed to Red Tories because it gave everyone a shot at equal opportunity. The small White House policy unit for this welfare reform was headed by Donald Rumsfeld and included Richard Cheney and Patrick Moynihan in their younger and more idealistic days.

At a formal luncheon address to the Empire Club at the Royal York Hotel on October 2, 1969, in advance of the Niagara conference, Stanfield stated the case in his usual thoughtful but focused way: "You may know that I have expressed the opinion that a successful welfare programme must emphasize three principles. First, it must try to see that every Canadian will have the opportunity of a decent standard of living. Secondly, it must make sure that public welfare funds are not given away unnecessarily to people who don't need help. Thirdly (and I emphasize this in particular) it must incorporate a system of incentives, a plan that positively encourages a man to get out and work as soon as possible."

Because of what had been reported in the press and in Republican circles about the progress being made by the Nixon White House on the Family Benefits Plan, Stanfield poked fun at those who seemed more concerned with labels than with substance: "Now some people are quick to apply labels to any new concept and refer to something like this as 'guaranteed annual income' or something of that sort; but I hope that in this country we can examine each other's principles and policies and their merits without becoming too distracted by semantics or with trying to drag too many red herrings across the trail. I hope we won't have to answer charges that Stanfield is going to pay everybody an income and that I am ladling out the free stuff. People who feel that way are sure lucky that the Conservative Party does not have a real dangerous radical as its leader – like Richard Nixon for example."

At the Niagara conference, Stanfield was more reserved in his support for a GAI, even though David MacDonald presented a paper in defence of it. As journalist Joyce Fairbairn reported in the *Winnipeg Free Press*, the party's "Thinkers Conference" endorsed a broad overhaul of the Canadian welfare system but rejected a universal guaranteed annual income.

The conference decided to strike a committee that would meld the GAI proposal and the opposition from the far right into a softer commitment to welfare reform, which left the door open. It asked the able and erudite former MP Jean Casselman Wadds to chair the committee. (Wadds, who hailed from Prescott, Ontario, would serve as high commissioner to London when Joe Clark briefly became prime minister in 1979.) This sort of resolution was emblematic of the sometimes oxymoronic nature of the Progressive Conservative Party. I recall vividly that Alberta MPs such as Jack Horner led the attack against the GAI concept. The irrepressible George Hees, who chaired the conference's unavoidable caucus committee on policy, joined with Stanfield and Horner in praising Wadds's excellent effort at reaching compromise and common ground.

The idea of a GAI had emerged at the Niagara conference but not been endorsed. Nonetheless, media coverage of the debate was extensive, and the GAI concept had made an impact on me. I saw the GAI as an idea whose time had come, but it had been set aside for lack of courage by the party in which I believed. I consoled myself, without a shred of justifying evidence, that Mr. Diefenbaker would not have stood down from the GAI. And the kernel of the idea for a less stigmatizing top-up for poor Canadians was firmly in place now, if not yet in the party platform.

My paternal grandfather, Benjamin Segal, at his sewing table in a factory. A tailor and a shop steward for the International Ladies' Garment Workers' Union (ILGWU), he identified with the plight of working men and women who, like himself, had only piecework, unpredictable wages, and no benefits of any kind.

My parents, Sadye Dankner and Morris Jack Segal, on their wedding day in 1937.

At our dining room table on rue Jeanne-Mance in 1951. My mother holds me on her lap next to my oldest brother, Seymour.

High school graduation photo, 1968. I am fourth from the right in the bottom row. When Joan Baez came to Montreal as part of a tour protesting the Vietnam War, Mr. Candib, the headmaster of Herzliah High School (centre, top right) suggested that we send a smoked fish platter to her hotel room (as she was a known vegetarian) so that we might interview her. It worked, and Baez graciously let us interview her for an hour. She was elegant, courteous, and kind.

FACING PAGE:
Out and about in the neighbourhood at age five in my hand-me-down jacket, 1954.

My bar mitzvah photo, October 1963.

Prime Minister John Diefenbaker speaking at a school in Cranbrook, BC, May 26, 1962. When Diefenbaker spoke at our school, his words lit a pilot light inside of me. Life was not just about the next year of school or what I planned to do that summer. It was about finding a purpose above and beyond that, about the role even a kid from a lower-working-class family might be able to play. *Columbia Basin Institute of Regional History*

David MacDonald and I (centre) examine lobster traps in Tignish, PEI, in 1970, with a lobster fisher (left) and Nathan Nurgitz, then president of the PC Party of Canada (right). I worked as a volunteer in David MacDonald's Ottawa office, starting in 1969. MacDonald, who was also a United Church minister, represented the PEI riding of Egmont and was a key member of the progressive Red Tory left of the party.

Flyer from my campaign when I ran as the PC candidate for Ottawa Centre in the 1972 federal election.

The caption in this Canadian Press photo reads, "Hugh Segal, federal Progressive Conservative candidate in Ottawa Centre, settles down in an Ottawa shoe store on Wednesday, May 17, 1972, for a re-shoeing after canvassing 2,500 homes in his riding since early March." *The Canadian Press / Peter Bregg*

Campaigning down Bronson Avenue in Ottawa Centre during the 1974 federal election with Claude Wagner (right), MP for Saint-Hyacinthe and PC shadow minister of foreign affairs. His son Richard is now chief justice of the Supreme Court of Canada.

Robert Stanfield, leader of the Opposition, 1972. The best prime minister we never had. I had the privilege of joining Stanfield's staff in the early 1970s, eventually becoming his legislative secretary. Mr. Stanfield was an early promoter of a guaranteed annual income, and I came to see him as the personification of the "progressive" in Progressive Conservative. *The Canadian Press / Ted Grant*

William Davis, then education minister, speaking at a Conservative rally in Toronto, beneath a portrait of Premier John Robarts, 1970. *Toronto Star / Dick Darrell*

Premiers Bill Davis (left) and Richard Hatfield admire six-week-old Jacqueline Sadye Armstrong Segal, held by her mother, my partner, Donna Armstrong Segal, at Robertson's Point, New Brunswick, 1982.

Premier Bill Davis (right) visiting a daycare centre, around 1978. The inscription on the photo reads, "Hugh, this is what government is all about." I would become deeply impressed with both Davis and his brand of conservatism. *Toronto Star*

From 1981 to 1983, I had the privilege of participating in patriation negotiations for Canada's Constitution as Ontario's associate cabinet secretary for federal-provincial affairs. Pictured here during a pause in the negotiations are Premier Bill Davis (left), federal constitutional affairs minister Jean Chrétien, and me.

I worked with Brian Mulroney as a volunteer in his 1984 and 1988 federal election campaigns, then as a senior policy advisor, and ultimately as his chief of staff. We are pictured here and with Mila Mulroney (below) in the Centre Block Office in 1992. Brian Mulroney always led with his heart, whether the issue was bilingualism, the Constitution, human rights, apartheid, the fight against Iraqi aggression against Kuwait, or land agreements with First Nations. Though never without risks, he chose a courageous course for Canada and the world.

In 1993, I returned to the School of Policy Studies at Queen's University, headed by Keith Banting. Now professor emeritus there, Keith was senior researcher director on the Macdonald Royal Commission, which recommended both free trade and a guaranteed annual income. He was also a member of the Opposition research office under the leadership of Robert Stanfield, when the issue of a guaranteed annual income first came up.

In 1998, I was a candidate for the leadership of the federal Tories. My leadership campaign was spirited and policy-focused, including a proposal for a basic income policy. However, the party was inclined to give Joe Clark a second chance. *The Canadian Press / John Lehmann*

In 2009, I was nominated by the Department of Foreign Affairs and International Trade to sit as the Canadian representative on the Commonwealth Eminent Persons Group (EPG). In this photo, EPG members flank the queen in Buckingham Palace. From left, Samuel Kavuma from Uganda, Patricia Francis from Jamaica, Sir Ieremia Tabai from Kiribati, Tun Abdullah Ahmad Badawi from Malaysia, Secretary-General Kamalesh Sharma, me, Dr. Asma Jahangir from Pakistan, Sir Malcolm Rifkind from Britain, Sir Ronald Sanders from Antigua and Barbuda, and Michael Kirby from Australia, July 20, 2010. *The Canadian Press / John Stillwell*

From 2005 to 2014, it was my honour to serve in the Canadian Senate. Throughout my time there, various issues and debates drew me in, but I admit to shamelessly using my Senate position as a podium to champion a GAI, in an attempt to sway those who had the real clout in shaping policy. Here I am, making the case for the GAI in Calgary in 2012.

As principal of Massey College, I had many duties. Here I am greeting students in the Visitor's Office in 2017. The office originally belonged to the Rt. Hon. Vincent Massey, a founder of the college. *Photographed by Jim Rankin*

Here I am speaking at a Massey High Table dinner, which was held twice monthly in the Oxbridge fashion. My final speech at the Senior Fellows Luncheon in 2019 was titled "Massey College: Change, Tradition, and Civility in a More Complex World." *Photographed by Dhoui Chang*

Rosemarie Brisson and I at Queen's University in June of 2017, when I received an honorary doctorate.

In March 2017, Premier Kathleen Wynne announced the launch of the basic income pilot project in Hamilton, Ontario. Hamilton, Thunder Bay, and Lindsay were designated test sites with the goal of involving four thousand Ontario residents. *The Canadian Press / Dave Chidley*

Former premier Kathleen Wynne shows her support for basic income in November 2018, despite the pilot project's cancellation by the newly elected Conservative government earlier that year. *From* Humans of Basic Income, A Portrait Series *by Jessie Golem*

A poster for an event supporting a basic income pilot project event in Toronto, 2017.
Thomas Threndyle (graphic artist), courtesy St. Andrew's Church

Protestors at an August 2018 rally in Lindsay's Victoria Park decry the provincial government's decision to prematurely end the basic income pilot project. *Torstar / Bill Hodgins*

CHAPTER 8

Sinews of Impunity

▼

In the end we will remember not the words of
our enemies but the silence of our friends.

MARTIN LUTHER KING

▲

IN OCTOBER 1970, I woke up one morning to see Canadian Forces armoured
personnel carriers stationed on the University of Ottawa campus in the
parking lot beside the student union building on Laurier Avenue East
near Sacré-Coeur Church. In the middle of the night of October 16, the
Trudeau government had proclaimed the War Measures Act (WMA). I was
the president of a student union at a university occupied, however gently,
by the Canadian Armed Forces.

I had been following the escalation of anxiety in Quebec and Ottawa
that rolled out after an FLQ cell kidnapped James Cross, a British trade
commissioner, from his Montreal residence and then kidnapped Quebec
labour minister Pierre Laporte while he tossed a football around in front
of his home with his children. Laporte was subsequently murdered. The
government of Robert Bourassa looked anything but strong and resolute.
The provincial justice minister, Jérôme Choquette, seemed awash in
bluster, with little result. The police forces in Montreal and Quebec City
and the Quebec Provincial Police (now the Sûreté du Québec) all seemed
flummoxed and were very soon in advanced stages of burnout. The
Quebec media, though united against any use of violence, were not

completely unsympathetic to the poverty and unjust working conditions faced by many in the province, which clearly drove the hard-left class-warfare side of the independence movement.

In the 1968 election, Pierre Trudeau had done well in Quebec, but grievances long part of the *revendications traditionnelles du Québec* remained in some measure unaddressed. René Lévesque had left Quebec's Liberal government to begin the early version of the Parti Québécois (PQ). Claude Ryan, editor-in-chief of the nationalist newspaper *Le Devoir,* though not a separatist, was no fan of the rigid centralism of the federal Liberals, and neither was his paper. Bob Stanfield and most provincial premiers favoured the *fédéralisme rentable* (flexible federalism) approach coined by Prime Minister Pearson to facilitate the spread of universal health insurance from Saskatchewan to the rest of Canada, agreement on the Canada Pension Plan, and agreement on post-secondary funding. Generally, Conservatives believed that section 92 of the British North America Act, which set out provincial powers, was as salient as section 91 on federal powers.

Invoking the War Measures Act, a bill passed by Parliament in 1914 to deal with the threat of war and subversion and to manage other pressures internally, was a very muscular over-reaction to what was effectively two criminal offences and lots of high-strung rhetorical histrionics from a tiny group of extreme revolutionaries. It was the old hammer-for-a-fly response. The police were under desperate pressure to find the perpetrators. Some "swells" in the more nationalist Québécois labour, business, academic, journalistic, and political circles suggested that Premier Bourassa shape a new cabinet made up of an all-talents group of self-styled prominent folks that would span the full federalist-sovereigntist spectrum. *Le Devoir,* the historic journal of nationalist thought and arts, ran with the idea.

Trudeau had dispatched senior officials to Quebec to convince Bourassa and the mayor of Montreal to sign letters calling for the War Measures Act. At the end of their tether, with the police at their own wit's end, that is precisely what they did. The fiction of a spontaneous request for help from Quebec was sustained in this way. In fact, it was a curated request, reflecting Ottawa's desire to use force.

And so the deployments of armed Canadian troops in the streets of Ottawa, Montreal, and Quebec City began. As did the de jure end of civil liberties for all Canadians while the WMA was in effect. Its strict application was in Quebec, but the federal nature of the law as proclaimed meant that, in principle, civil liberties could be proscribed all across Canada – something Premier John Robarts of Ontario was surprised and angry to discover. Freedom of assembly, freedom of association, freedom of expression, and freedom of the press were gone, signed away by a proclamation in the middle of the night.

Those who were arrested under the WMA were also surprised and angry. They were not involved in kidnapping or murder or anything like a broad conspiracy to break the law. Instead, they were alleged to be members of, or sympathetic to, organizations banned by the WMA and its proclamation. The federal government had decided that the way to end the crisis was to arrest as many members of the *contestateur* class of Québécois as possible.

In addition, the proclamation made it illegal to disclose the contents of the FLQ Manifesto – which had already been circulated widely and broadcast by Radio Canada at the demand of the FLQ itself. Police officers who – thankfully – had no training in how to muzzle the basic freedoms of speech, assembly, and the press were nonetheless deployed to do so.

The University of Ottawa had a large Québécois student body, many of whom were separatist in inclination (and all of whom opposed the Vietnam War). Political clubs for the PCs, the Liberals, the NDP, and the PQ had their offices in the student union building where I worked. All these clubs were registered with the university and were quite legal. This, however, did not stop two police officers from visiting our building, skipping all the offices except for the PQ's, rifling through its drawers, and carrying out boxes of files and members' names. The officers, following orders set somewhere else, were friendly and a little unclear as to why they were doing what they were doing. But they were doing it anyway.

Of course, I was not opposed to following the law, but I was certainly opposed to this law. If there were evidence of criminal conspiracy to commit a crime, plant a bomb, or violate the law, that was one thing. But in the absence of violations, mass arrests struck me as a more serious threat to democracy than whatever the FLQ cells might have in mind, let alone what they could actually do. (I would learn years later in my work as chair of the Senate Committee on Anti-Terrorism that there is a big difference between intent and capacity, a difference that competent criminal intelligence or strategic intelligence forces should lawfully be able to determine.)

The deputy solicitor general had telephoned Father Guindon, our rector, to inform him that, because the campus was so close to Parliament Hill and many of the official ambassadorial residences were in Rockcliffe and on Range Road, the university would be under intense scrutiny. No violation of the WMA would be tolerated. Both Guindon and I wondered what might produce that kind of paranoia in response to two kidnappings and one murder in a country where more people died in car accidents every day. But we had been warned. As president of the student body, I encouraged students to follow the new law, and I chaired a public meeting at the university with legal counsel present to clearly explain what it meant. I did not want to see student careers ruined by a capricious arrest.

About a week into the WMA, with arrests rolling out throughout Quebec, mostly in Montreal, I was visited by a young Québécois student who was doing his honours in French literature in the Faculty of Arts. His problem? Unhappily, he and one of the kidnappers of James Cross shared the same name. The student was worried that this coincidence (the two men were not related or connected in any way) might result in his arrest. Our legal counsel suggested that he go down to Ottawa police headquarters and identify himself so the local authorities would know that he was who he said he was. The counsel, who was chair of our student union grand council, a senior law student in the Faculty of Common Law, and the son of a retired member of the RCMP Security and Intelligence unit, agreed to accompany the student for that formality.

In a perfect example of what happens when unconstitutional laws are passed, setting aside Magna Carta principles that should protect the common law precedent of presumption of innocence and habeas corpus, the young student, who did not have a political bone in his body, was immediately detained at the police station. Our legal counsel was told that the matter no longer concerned him and informed that he should leave the station unless he wished to be detained himself. He was furious, and so was I. When I spoke on the phone with the student's mother, her anguish was completely understandable. We learned later that he had been shipped to a police holding centre deep in the Gatineau region.

I called MP David MacDonald. He said he would raise the matter at the Question Period planning session that took place every morning in the Opposition lobby on Parliament Hill, which he did. As a result, Robert Stanfield, leader of Her Majesty's Loyal Opposition, rose in his seat to ask the prime minister where this young man was, why he had been arrested, and when he would be released. Trudeau, whose office had been given notice of the question that morning, replied, reasonably, that though he did not know, he would be glad to look into the matter and report back.

Like the young student, hundreds had been arrested. Many were held for days without ever being formally charged with a crime. Pierre Marc Johnson, a young law student, the son of former Union Nationale premier Daniel Johnson, was arrested and released five times. This was a capricious, uninformed use of unconstitutional arrest as a source of fear, intimidation, and raw power. People were arrested because of some possible vague political association, not only with the sovereigntist movement, but with any group in Quebec that openly advocated more fairness, less poverty, the cleaning up of corruption, better working conditions, or even the increased unionization of work sites. It was Pierre Trudeau at his arrogant, insensitive worst, and not one of the senior officials or ministers involved in this wildly anti-democratic conspiracy to arrest hundreds was ever held accountable. In 1976, the Parti Québécois would win a resounding victory over the Bourassa administration, and Quebec was henceforth democratically in the hands of those committed to its separation from Canada. Many lower-income parts of the province firmly voted PQ. The young literature student who had been arrested under the War Measures Act for being honest volunteered in the PQ campaign in Hull during that election, a seat the party won after decades of Liberal domination.

For me, at age twenty, the invocation of the WMA was a vivid example of how lawlessness can be perpetuated by the state in ways that can do more damage than the evil the state is seeking to control. The fact that many of those arrested were student activists, kids classically on the left side of politics, with or without a sovereigntist tinge, was further indication of what happens when honest police officers are asked to do something that contravenes their "serve and protect" mission. As a Tory, as an active member in the PCSF, I opposed many of the hard-left, sovereigntist opinions routinely expressed on campus. But I held the naive view that

Canadian sailors, soldiers, and fliers had fought and died all over the world to defend the rights of Canadians to freedom of expression and freedom of the press. I concluded that the present batch of federal Liberals left no room for dissent and saw the use of force to crush engaged non-violent opposition as quite all right. I remembered that, in 1948, only a few years before the anti-communist McCarthy excesses in the United States, John Diefenbaker, not yet party leader, had blocked a Conservative policy proposal to outlaw the Communist Party in Canada.

Other important pieces would unfold as the WMA continued. It was clear that English Canadians were delighted with Trudeau's hardline stance, and his party's popularity soared to over 70 percent. Robert Stanfield faced a serious challenge. His instincts were to oppose Trudeau's authoritarian decision, but he knew that the PC Party would splinter into smithereens if he did. So he took the reasonable stance of giving the government the benefit of the doubt while asking questions daily in the House and trying to hold the Liberals accountable for their actions. With the government doing the old "if you knew what we knew, all of which we can't tell you" routine, the media, with few exceptions, sadly rolled over. Only three Anglo journalists of standing spoke up for the rule of law and the Constitution – the irrepressible George Bain, columnist for the *Globe and Mail*; Peter Riley, then anchor of the local CTV newscast; and Tim Raife, a Parliament Hill reporter for the CBC. Tommy Douglas and his NDP caucus had voted against the War Measures Act, which caused the party's support to erode by a third. Even Stanfield's loyal equivocation reduced his party's standing by 50 percent.

In frustration at the closed-shop approach to public debate and discussion, David MacDonald, Flora MacDonald, and a few others decided to issue a booklet of reasoned articles, questioning the need for and appropriateness of the WMA. Its writers spanned the spectrum. David MacDonald wrote on the parliamentary context. Dian Cohen, the famous economist, wrote about the economic circumstances in Quebec, and Jim Littleton, a CBC producer and writer, covered the shady area of what terrorism in Quebec was and was not. Nate Nurgitz, a distinguished lawyer and former magistrate in Winnipeg, who was also the PC national vice-president from the Prairies, wrote about how the Coroner's Act actually provided all the powers the state needed to hold witnesses and get the facts, obviating the more extreme powers of the WMA. Patrick Watson, the distinguished CBC journalist (and future chair of the CBC under Brian Mulroney), contributed a piece about how the Opposition had failed in its duties to oppose. Claude Parisée wrote in French about the targeting and humiliation of the labour movement. Peter Desbarats addressed police adequacy issues. The distinguished historian James Eayrs traced Canada's history of internment of lawful citizens during wartime, and I contributed a piece about how Trudeau had lost the moderates on our campuses.

The booklet, which was entitled *Strong and Free: Nos Foyers et Nos Droits; A Response to the War Measures Act,* had a sketch of a soldier on the cover. The little pamphlet spoke of the difficult realities of poverty, the low standard of living in many parts of Quebec, and the relationship between this poverty, the exclusionary nature of government in both Ottawa and Quebec City, and the unavoidable manifestation of greater nationalism within Quebec as a result. No writer showed even a faint interest in encouraging violence of any kind.

David MacDonald and I found a small printer on Daly Avenue in Ottawa (called, if you can believe it, Bonanza Press), whose owner, Mr. Cartwright – an American with a broad Texas accent – was not afraid of the provisions of the War Measures Act. Flora MacDonald and others worked the phones to find a hundred people who would donate to cover the cost of printing and circulation. David and I took out a loan from the Bank of Montreal on the corner of Wellington and O'Connor to pay the printing costs up front. The list of financial contributors would today read like a who's who of business and political life. It included young lawyers Alan Eagleson and Roy McMurtry, advertising men Norman Atkins and Dalton Camp, and H.H. Stevens, the former Conservative minister who had created the Reconstructionist Party in the 1930s because more needed to be done for the poor. Among the other donors listed on the back cover, representing supporters from right across the country, were Lloyd Axworthy, Tom Berger, Claude Bissell, June Callwood, John Carter, Brian Flemming, Léo Dorais, MP Gordon Fairweather, Eddie Goodman, Wally Fox-Decent, George Grant, Tom Hockin, Hubert Guindon, James Laxer, William Macadam, James Macaulay, Michael Oliver, Abraham Rotstein, MP Doug Roland, William Saywell, Lloyd Shaw, Denis Stairs, George Perlin, Marcel Pepin, and Robert McClure. Economists, former moderators of the United Church, lawyers, business school professors, journalists, philosophers, authors – spanning the full spectrum of politics – had the courage to come forward.

The risk of donating, when there was no way of knowing where the government's next arrest surge might lead, was not insubstantial. Many of these donors, who agreed to have their names listed on the back of the booklet, wanted their opposition to the War Measures Act to be known. It speaks well of Canada that many went on to very high posts in academe, elected government, business, national security, journalism, various religious denominations, the judiciary, and the public service.

On December 1, the Public Order Act, a continuation of the WMA, was brought into effect. When it came to Parliament, the new act would have passed unanimously but for one MP who stood against it – the only one, the Reverend David MacDonald, MP for Egmont, Prince Edward Island. His rationale? Since the government had yet to prove the necessity of invoking the WMA, there was no justification whatever for its continuance with the Public Order Act. Although the NDP had opposed the War Measures Act, it did not oppose its temporary extension by Justice Minister John Turner.

▼

These two years were a steep learning curve for me. By the middle of 1971, I had had the rare opportunity of participating in discussions about international conflict in Africa and about a new approach to conservatism in Canada. I had volunteered as a researcher in David MacDonald's office and learned much about the social and economic challenges faced by his constituents in rural Prince Edward Island. I had joined the reasoned and lawful opposition to the WMA and seen what parliamentary courage and principle really meant. At the Niagara conference, I had witnessed a fulsome debate on a GAI, inspired by a genuine desire to eradicate poverty and modulated by classic tensions between the hard right and the centre-right wings of the party. The imprint of all this would develop over time. But what I remember as most salient were the linkages between poverty, freedom, international instability, order, and the sinews of our Canadian democracy. It all strengthened my conviction that politics was about improving the lives of others, especially those at the bottom of the economic chain. It was about making room at the family table, including for those with whom you disagreed. However imperfect, the Progressive Conservative Party, informed by the populism of Diefenbaker, the civility of Stanfield, and the courage of people such as David MacDonald, was obviously the place to do it.

CHAPTER 9

Learning from the Best

▼

Power has only one duty – to secure
the social welfare of the people.

BENJAMIN DISRAELI

▲

SO MUCH OF WHAT I discovered about the purpose of politics at its best
came from my days as an unpaid volunteer and then a paid second typist
in David MacDonald's Ottawa office. (This was before MP office budgets
accommodated actual research assistants.) That was followed by the
constituency work I did in his Egmont riding. I helped to translate the
day-to-day realities of life on its farms and fishing communities into
questions posed in the House of Commons, into representations to
ministers and departments, and into motions by David at organizational
meetings that spanned everything from the Horticultural Council (which
dealt with potato issues) to world federalists seeking a more rational
international order.

That MacDonald operated with an intrinsic mix of humanity, skill,
can-do optimism, infectious idealism, and inspired naiveté was generally
appreciated. His style and commitment defied any normative view of
the self-seeking politician on the make. David seemed to be the real-life
personification of the lead character in the 1960s CBC TV drama series
Quentin Durgens, M.P., starring the remarkable Gordon Pinsent. Except

that David was kind and engaged in ways that made the TV character seem small and self-centred by comparison.

I learned that there was a brutal reality to rural poverty, masked only on occasion by the bucolic red-earth countryside of beautiful Prince Edward Island. The issues were as diverse as what happened when a lobster boat licence was used on two boats on different PEI coasts to benefit from both seasons or who would get harvesting leases to gather carrageenan, a seaweed of great value in the Japanese market. How might funds be raised for Lennox Island, the centre of the island's First Nations community? Where might funds be found for Abrams Village, the Acadian community, with its schools, its community centre, and its cultural and language preservation activities?

When I joined David's staff in Ottawa, MPs had very moderate office allowances. Usually, two MPs shared one secretary and a relatively small office. Paid constituency offices in the home riding that functioned as an extension of the MP's Ottawa office were not in place when David was first elected in 1965. Nor did the government pay for long-distance telephone use. Constituents could write to their MPs without using a stamp – and that was deemed to be quite sufficient.

I distinctly remember negotiating with the good people of Bell Canada when my boss was a few weeks late in paying the long-distance charges for calls to and from his constituency. Long-distance was expensive back then, and many constituents who were in difficulty would call collect from a party line in the riding. David's small parliamentary salary, with an even smaller expense allowance, had to cover his constituency expenses, his home in Alberton, and the cost of his family home in Ottawa, on Wilbrod Street in Sandy Hill.

My own precarious financial situation meant that I did not buy my first men's suit retail until my third year of university. I got it on sale at Tip Top Tailors, then located on the Sparks Street Mall. During my high school years, any such need had been addressed in the back of some clothing factory on the Main in Montreal, where a cash transaction on a Saturday morning enabled my dad to pick a horrific suit from the seconds rack, usually from the "boys' husky" section. One such suit had a truly noxious light-grey flecked pattern, but at least the pants and jacket matched.

Having had the experience of buying my first suit retail, I noticed that David MacDonald's "three" suits (all worn and threadbare) often did not have matching slacks and jacket. Walking with him to the CBC studio in the National Press Building one day, I mentioned that Tip Top was having a sale. He could get a matching set for a really good price. David smiled. "Hugh, many of my constituents do not have a single suit, let alone one with a matching top and bottom. Those are the folks who sent me here, so I'm just fine. Let's talk about something important."

To serve people in genuine need, David understood, things had to be done differently. He created and instituted the first mobile constituency office of any Canadian MP. It was a second-hand yellow school bus (formerly from the Ottawa-based Uncle Harry's School Bus line) that David had painted grey and decorated with a large Canadian coat of arms on each side. The decals were thanks to the Air Canada lobbyist Hugh Riopelle, who got them from the airline. The bus was outfitted with a couple of desks, comfortable chairs, and a couch. After David drove it from Ottawa to Prince Edward Island, it was parked according to a published schedule in communities from Summerside to Tignish and all spots in between. People booked appointments in the usual way or simply showed up when the bus was parked in a shopping centre or schoolyard near where they lived. The office had a water cooler, a teapot always on the run, and a private spot in the back where David and a constituent could discuss the problem du jour. Back in Ottawa, it was often my job to research a program or check out the status of a veteran's land grant, a farming subsidy, or a passport application. Information was faxed or dictated over the expensive phone lines. David's engagement with, and advocacy for, farmers, fishing families, low-income seniors, veterans, people with disabilities, and others in his flock produced advocacy on vital related public policy projects back in Ottawa.

David fought for local consultation and flexibility in the much-vaunted PEI Comprehensive Development Plan, announced by the Liberal government. You did not have to be a PEI separatist to understand viscerally that broad-brushstroke plans shaped and funded in Ottawa might not be well suited to the ways in which folks dealt with unemployment, poverty, seasonal variations in prices, and tourism flows in the province. PEI premier Alex Campbell, a bright and genial Liberal, had the best interests of islanders at heart. But bureaucracies hundreds of miles away could detach from those interests and seek mega-development solutions that did not always address local needs.

I became a regular consumer of the CBC daily farm broadcast. Through David's advocacy, I understand today the complex math that determined the number of refrigerator cars (reefer cars) made available to the island by the railway and the mobility of the economically central potato crop off the island. A classic cycle would see him meet with the PEI Farmers' Union branch on the weekend, come back to Ottawa with its concerns, call the minister of agriculture, and if the issue were pressing, make a motion or statement in the House by Friday morning. I would call the text of the statement into the daily *Summerside Journal Pioneer,* talking directly to Elmer Murphy, its reasonably genial editor-in-chief (who was also the publisher, the main ad sales guy, and the rest). The story would appear on the front page of the Saturday issue, along with a picture of David and an image of reefer cars on a PEI siding.

When the Liberal government introduced the Opportunities for Youth Program (OFY) under Prime Minister Trudeau and Secretary of State Gérard Pelletier, Robert Stanfield appointed David as its shadow cabinet critic. I took this as licence to talk with the minister's executive assistant, Denise Robert, and hammer out a kind of "balanced civility" approach, whereby our questions in the Chamber and at committee would be "ad factum" – about the content and operations of OFY. They would not be about partisan motivation and thus would avoid the acerbic lines of questioning that Opposition critics often liked to pursue. (For example, Tom Cossit, MP for Leeds, fixated on the cost of the new toilets installed during a modest update to the plumbing at 24 Sussex Drive. Other Tory MPs fulminated over the cost of running the government's JetStar fleet of small planes for VIP travel.) My arrangement with Denise was straight-forward. Our office would take a substantive line and would not seek to uncover favouritism or unfairness in OFY. We would assume that the minister was doing his best to be balanced and even-handed. I made it softly clear that the balance and fairness shown to OFY in relation to Prince Edward Island would have a lot to do with how we saw things generally.

David, not surprisingly, viewed OFY as a way to provide summer jobs for young people in farming, fishing, and First Nations and low-income communities to help them break out of poverty and build more robust working opportunities throughout their lives. He also wanted this for communities and young people right across Canada.

We went to bat for Lennox Island, Abrams Village, tourism, and skills development. David reached out to high schools, the University of Prince Edward Island, Holland College, local chambers of commerce, and 4H clubs to get as broad a net of applications as possible. We even arranged for Denise Robert to come down to the island, rent a small unit at Blanche Edward's Cottages, not far from David's home in Alberton, and visit local projects.

David also worked with provincial ministers, regardless of party, to get supportive funding, advocating for every lower-income part of the country. The loyalty of islanders to each other far outstripped any partisan fealty. The notion of setting aside steel-toed partisanship to work together for common good was something I learned from David, and I also saw how much it helped his constituents. Letting partisan excess get in the way of good government could lead only to bad government, more waste, and poorer results for people in genuine need. Opposition parties who concentrate solely on attacking the government surrender half their mandate and a lot of their responsibility for upholding our democratic way of life. Measured opposition is always of value, but opposing as a way of life becomes both soul destroying and a self-fulfilling prophesy.

Pierre Trudeau's slim majority in 1968 had been, in some respects, a response not only to his personal appeal and popularity but also to public fatigue with the incessant hyper-partisanship of Diefenbaker and Pearson, which diminished both leaders, their parties, and the legitimacy of the system overall. This was a lesson I would keep with me all my life. David MacDonald's willingness to work with and alongside anyone, regardless of political stripe, also showed me that the causes of poverty and its associated pathologies defy any partisan analysis. Canada's federal-provincial division of powers argues for governments to work across partisan divides with some unity of purpose. Failure on that front reduces the salience of responsible government and the very legitimacy of democracy itself.

After being elected to Parliament, David continued to take over rural charges within the United Church in his riding when ministers went on holiday, were ill, or simply had to be away, arguing that it made him a better MP. He invited me to do the odd first draft of a sermon, and suffice

it to say that his addresses over those two summers had a touch more
Old Testament imagery and tone.

▼

I was elected national vice-president of the Progressive Conservative
Student Federation (PCSF) in December 1971, at a convention held in the
basement of the Anglican cathedral, across the street from the National
Library.

Since arriving in Ottawa, I had been active in young Conservative
circles in the area as well as on campus. After supporting Bill Davis in the
Tory provincial leadership convention earlier that year, I had introduced
him at a rally in Ottawa South as the new Ontario PC leader. I had campaigned for the government's re-election in October 1971. A few folks had
also heard of me because of my public engagement on the War Measures
Act, essentially against extremism on both sides.

But I was still surprised when Alan Pope, the outgoing PCSF president,
called to encourage me to run for the national vice-presidency. Darwin
Kealey, a member of the PCSF executive and an organizer for the party,
with eastern Ontario roots, also called to engage me. I knew that another
candidate, Jack Houseman, an active PCSF militant for many years, was
already in the race, with the support of Sean O'Sullivan, a fabled youth
leader and prospective MP on the party's right. So, just two weeks before
the leadership convention, I entered the contest with a "nothing ventured,
nothing gained" approach. When I expressed my "late to the race" concerns,
Alan and Darwin urged me to make the best speech I could about what a
political party was for and what kinds of policies PC students should be
advocating. When it was my turn at the podium, I proposed a policy process that was more open and considered, less secretive, and more reflective of genuine community needs than the current norm. Low-income
people, students in financial trouble, farmers, small-business people, and
new immigrants, I suggested, were the natural constituents of a new
and larger Progressive Conservative Party. Our support for the Crown,
Confederation, and parliamentary democracy had to be matched by the
courage to innovate and to engage on narrowing the gap between rich

and poor. I also argued for a PCSF-wide policy process that would be open to every campus and, someday, to high schools across Canada.

I was truly surprised to win. The new president was Len Domino, a scrappy, bright, hard-working community organizer from the working-class Transcona part of Winnipeg. Neither he nor I had ever really seen a silver spoon, let alone been born with one in our mouths. Ours was an interesting point of departure. Together, we would attempt to broaden the organization, striving to develop an urbane and progressive party platform that would attract more than small-town and rural white males who were over the age of fifty, the usual default constituency for Canadian Conservatives.

Part of my role as the national vice-president was to represent the PCSF in platform and policy discussions during the lead-up to the 1972 election. The resulting circumstances were unexpected, to say the least. My new mission brought me into regular contact with the Progressive Conservative Policy Coordinating Committee, chaired by the estimable, deeply thoughtful, highly intellectual Tom Symons, president of the still young Trent University. Tom has been a wondrous pillar/mentor for my own more modest intellectual and public policy life ever since. His function at the committee was discharged with a mix of finesse, tough-minded focus, and diplomatic acuity. The committee met in PC head-quarters at 178 Laurier in Ottawa, a setting replete with noisy plumbing and spotty heating – but it was what the party could afford. Tom sat at his end of the table with an array of silver Thermoses containing tea. He smoked a pipe, filling it at strategic points in the meetings. He kept folks from opposite ends of the conservative spectrum engaging even when fisticuffs seemed unavoidable. He managed to produce a range of policy direction papers that tilted the party onto a progressive path while leaving the leader's options for tactical platform choices wide open. Whatever I learned about how to run a meeting or chair a board, I learned by watching and absorbing Tom's dazzling intellectual and diplomatic methods. He was an academic leader who personified that much-maligned and disappearing quality, civility. That sense of civility and how to promote and maintain it stuck with me through every stage of my future work at Queen's Park, as a candidate for office or leadership, as a nationalist with an abiding concern for an inclusive Canadian sense of identity and pride, as chief of staff to a prime minister, as head of a think-tank, and as a member of public corporate and NGO boards.

Tom exemplified the notion that civility in public life didn't happen by accident. If it were to be achieved, its advocates and foot soldiers must dare the vicissitudes and risks of running for political office. It was while sitting at Tom's policy table that I decided to do my part in the struggle by seeking office myself. My commitment to that idea took the form of a desperate desire to run against Pierre Trudeau in my home riding of Mount Royal during the 1972 election.

I believed that Trudeau's deployment of the War Measures Act had been an unconstitutional attempt to shut down debate in a democracy and also to shut down the separatist cause. I was convinced that separatism should be confronted by a better idea, a vision of federalism that was buoyant and inclusive. I was firmly of the view by then that politically motivated violence was partially driven by social and economic injustice. Perhaps, I thought, my candidacy against the trust-fund-based dilettante, however slim my chances of defeating him, could make the case for a greater, more inclusive civility. Perhaps it would be the best way to promote broad appreciation of that principle, even in a "rotten borough." I knew from experience that though Mount Royal had corners of great wealth and standing, some parts of the riding were in no way immune to the ravages of poverty and hardship.

Luckily, my bold plan was deflected by the kind but focused attention of Barney London, a Maritimer and former head of Niagara Finance. As the Mount Royal riding president, he urged me to run in Ontario, where a Conservative might have a chance of actually winning. It took several meetings with Barney to discourage my lust for the Mount Royal candidacy and direct me elsewhere. Barney had the down-to-earth humanity and pragmatism that my sense of mission sorely lacked. "Losing your deposit in a totally safe Liberal seat, which even Diefenbaker couldn't win in the 1958 sweep, will serve no purpose," he told me. "Give your head a shake." I did, and he was very, very right.

As a student at the University of Ottawa, I realized that rural Ontario ridings where Tories had a chance of electoral victory already had a long queue of prospective and better-known candidates. They would not have room for a young aspirant with my limited qualifications. That led me to Ottawa Centre, a riding right in the heart of town, which was held by

George McIlraith, a long-serving Trudeau MP and Pearson government minister. Among other worthies, he had defeated Charlotte Whitton during the Diefenbaker sweep of 1958. She was the riding's PC candidate and a very popular mayor of Ottawa. Nonetheless, I thought I might have a chance of winning the PC nomination and beginning my struggle from there. Part of McIlraith's immovable electoral appeal had been his role as minister of public works, the ultimate source back then of jobs at all levels of the bureaucracy and the supplier to government trades in Ottawa. Loyalty throughout your region is much deeper when access to jobs is fundamental to your promise as the local MP and minister.

Working with Jerry Lampert, president of the Carleton University student government and a dear and reliable friend, I campaigned for the nomination on social and economic justice, building links with seniors and students in the riding. I eked out a first-ballot victory despite the well-qualified candidacies of Eddie Foster, a distinguished in-house counsel for Canadian Pacific, and Ian Doig, a well-established investment advisor. We simply out-organized and outflanked both of them. Winning that nomination in April 1972 involved will, determination, and intense door-to-door campaigning.

Going door to door brought me into direct contact with what mattered in the everyday lives of the voters whose support I eagerly sought. It also helped me to understand that the incoherence of public attitudes about poverty needed to be countered by the realities of the street-level poverty I confronted daily. I had campaigned for the nomination on several planks, including welfare reform. As leader, Stanfield was focusing on the poverty caused by the high unemployment rate of the day. In all-candidates meetings and debates, I talked about the need to make poverty a priority and outlined new ways, including a guaranteed income, of reducing its most serious effects on people, families, and communities. Liberal, NDP, and waffle candidates were surprised to hear a Tory head in that direction. But since I was the youngest by decades on the stage, they did not take my position, or me, very seriously.

My near win for the PC Party in 1972 (I lost by a mere 555 votes in a riding that the Liberals had repeatedly won by thousands of votes) created notice for my efforts, not only in Ottawa and the upper reaches of the party, but also at Queen's Park. I finished my undergraduate degree

that year, and after my surprising close finish, I was offered a job by
Graham Scott, Bob Stanfield's executive assistant, who had been a PCSF
leader and was a former university Naval Training Division lieutenant. As
appointments secretary to Stanfield (the most junior job in the office), I
got to help arrange the leader's schedule, and I was deeply honoured just
to be there. For all of us who worked for Robert Stanfield, the cycle was
the same. When you arrived, you looked around the office at the other,
far brighter people, with their vast experience, and wondered what you
were doing there. Then, when ego overtook judgment, and you noticed
how the caucus undermined Stanfield, you wondered what he was doing
there. Then, once you had a tiny bit of experience, you wondered how you
could ever leave when working for someone as bright, decent, concerned
for others, and measured as Bob Stanfield.

In 1972, the plight of the unemployed, along with Stanfield's championing of a guaranteed annual income, albeit through a soft platform
proposal of welfare reform, had helped the PC Party's prospects immensely.
So had the successful NDP campaign against "corporate welfare bums"
(companies that got taxpayers' money from Ottawa, while the poor lan-
guished). Trudeau's forty-plus polling lead was reduced to a bare two-seat
victory, a minority government, with the two seats being won by fewer
than ten votes. During the 1974 election, Stanfield's support for a ninety-
day freeze on prices and wages, to help seniors living on small pensions
that were ravaged by high inflation, put Ottawa Centre in a "likely Tory
win" category for the local media. Believing the kudos and clippings from
my 1972 near-miss, I ran again in 1974 against Hugh Poulin, the genial
lawyer and former McIlraith campaign manager who barely held Ottawa
Centre in the previous round.

But Trudeau's catchphrase "Zap! You're frozen" left our party's proposal
open to ridicule and rallied union members and civil servants to desert
the NDP and vote for the Liberals. It mattered not that civil servants and
unionized workers had salaried positions that would be untouched by the
proposed three-month freeze, whereas rents and prices would be constrained. Trudeau took his minority to a solid majority. A collapsed NDP
vote meant trouble for Tories everywhere, including Ottawa Centre. I lost
the riding by four thousand votes, despite increasing the Tory vote over
1972. The Tories had been bloodied by the electorate's fear of change; the

Liberals had been victorious by opposing change. I had been bloodied myself in the local political wars, and I was determined to seek another way forward. But I had learned some valuable lessons.

During my 1972 and 1974 election campaigns, I had spent much of my time going door to door in Ottawa Centre, which then covered the communities nestled between the Ottawa River on the north, the Rideau Canal on the east, the Rideau River on the south, and Carling Boulevard on the west. The riding was a diverse mix of wealthy, poor, and working class, civil servants, young professionals, and seniors, with anglophones, then francophones, then Italian Canadians and Lebanese Canadians as the pillar communities.

I was determined not to campaign solely in the leafy, relatively well-off districts of the Glebe, Clemow Avenue, and south Ottawa neighbourhoods. I believed that taking my case to low-income areas was both a duty and good politics. Ontario's guaranteed annual income supplement would not be initiated until 1975, yet I encountered many seniors who lived in desperate conditions, which became apparent as soon as they opened the door. I always campaigned with a volunteer, many of whom were from the neighbourhood. They might even know people's names and histories.

"Hugh," the volunteer would say to me, "this next door coming up is Agnes Turnbull, a woman in her seventies, a widow, not doing too well."

In response to our knock, Mrs. Turnbull would walk slowly to the door, and her warm smile would reveal many missing or rotting teeth. The state of her clothes spoke volumes. This was not a genteel way of life but a constrained one. This was poverty, a walk-up in Mechanicsville, in a damp three-storey building that seemed never to have been cleaned. Cigarette smoke soaked the corridors and was an even stronger odour when the apartment door opened. Often, the resident invited us in for a cup of tea. Strapped for time, we politely begged off, exchanged some pleasantries, handed over a pamphlet, asked if the person needed a ride to the polls, and, on occasion, answered a few questions.

The odd time, someone's reaction would go beyond the usual sarcasm or disinterest and have real bite.

"Hello, Mrs. Turnbull," I would say. "My name is Hugh Segal. I'm the PC candidate in the coming federal election. May I give you this pamphlet?"

"You guys are all the same. What are you gonna do for me, eh? You're just in it for yourselves."

Or, "Yeah, well, la di da, a Conservative in this part of town. Got nothing better to do? I wouldn't vote for you or anyone."

Or, "After the election in three weeks, this apartment will get very cold. What will you do for me then, eh?"

In those walk-ups, anger and cynicism seemed not one bit out of place. Nor were they out of place in a flat just north of Gloucester that housed five children, the oldest about eleven. We waited until about 7:30 p.m., after dinner, before knocking on that door, hoping the parents would be home from work. The oldest child opened the door. The mayhem behind her was obvious. "I'm sorry, my mom isn't home."

"Could I leave her this pamphlet for when she gets back?" I asked cheerfully.

"Won't be back till tomorrow morning, maybe," the girl reported. I handed her the pamphlet, mumbled something about the number to call if we could help on election day, thanked her, and moved on to the next door.

We often canvassed until nine, then headed back to HQ to find out how canvassers had done in other parts of the riding. Back at our committee rooms on Bronson, not far from the McNabb arena, we recorded what we had learned about rides to the polls, voter intention, and so on. There was no talk of anything else we had experienced. One evening, at about the three-week mark of a six-week drive, one of the canvassers offered, "This isn't a great neighbourhood for us. A lot of unemployment and welfare." This was said as though reporting the weather.

"Why does that mean we can't hope for any support?" I asked.

"Well, those areas tend not to vote Tory. They never have in this riding."

"Why?" I asked again, with all the naiveté of an earnest young candidate. "We say more about poverty than the other guys. Mr. Stanfield has raised poverty directly in the campaign. Why should we write off this part of the riding?"

"Well, it won't hurt us that much," the poll captain said. "The turnout in the poor districts is low anyway."

There it was, stated baldly for me to absorb. Poor people didn't vote as much as better-off people did. So why worry?

It was the ultimate discrimination of low expectations. Poor people were too obsessed with the day-to-day, with minimum-wage or welfare cheque-to-cheque survival to care enough to vote, so it was easier just to ignore them.

Something snapped later that night in my unable-to-sleep brain. We were running for office but not really believing that everyone would want to vote. The party spent most of its time in areas where voters were better off and actually going to the polls.

The next day, I got out census data that illustrated the income splits in Ottawa Centre versus those of tonier ridings such as Ottawa West. Parts of Sandy Hill or Vanier had poverty levels no better than the worst ones in my riding, although the Rockcliffe Park and New Edinburgh neighbourhoods were substantially better off. My riding had some wealthier sections, high-end highrises along the canal and leafy bits in the Glebe. But by and large, about 20 percent of Ottawa Centre residents lived beneath the poverty line as then defined.

My local organization was made up of students, long-time Tory volunteers, and some new joins who thought a young candidate was either a ray of sunshine or in desperate need of support. They wanted to focus our campaign on the wealthier areas that were most likely to vote Conservative. Why would they not?

I began to meet with the local clergy and neighbourhood volunteer groups, such as the Good Shepherd Hostel and the soup kitchens, to ask more about how people were living. I continued with the door-to-door canvassing, the all-candidates debates, the odd party rally, and the telephone calls for fundraising, but I was determined to understand the dynamic and texture of poverty in the seat I sought to serve in Parliament.

I was an enthusiastic supporter of my party's price and wage freeze because my door-to-door campaign had shown me what runaway inflation (then around 10 percent, three times or more than the present rate) was doing to food prices, rents, and people living on fixed incomes. Ontario had no rent control before the 1975 provincial election. In the end, for me, running in Ottawa Centre was really about wanting to help folks who were down on their luck.

I concluded a few things from my experience in 1974. Liberals could be better at campaigning than we were. Our price and incomes policy had too many shades of grey. And better-off people cast their ballots far more often than the poor. We needed to break through the barrier and allow the less well off some say, even though their lives demanded so much of a focus on simple subsistence that they didn't have time to care much about politics. If we didn't, we would be seeding the clouds for one hell of a big storm, not just in my riding, the province, or the country, but far beyond. I also concluded that coherence mattered. In the 1974 campaign, the PC Party championed various positions on the price and wage freeze. Stanfield and most candidates, including myself, supported a temporary ninety-day freeze on all prices and wages. Diefenbaker campaigned on freezing prices alone, not wages. Jack Horner, the MP in Crowfoot, had his own policy, as did James Gillies, the PC finance critic. This lack of consistency made us an easy target for the Liberals – how could a party that disagreed on its own policies possibly run the country? We had found a way to defeat ourselves, a Tory skill acquired over many years. In the end, competence and coherence matter as much as policy courage.

▼

In December 1974, I was asked to join the Bill Davis campaign committee in Toronto as campaign secretary, the most junior position in that organization. After several years on Stanfield's staff, culminating in the role of legislative secretary and a stint as a director of planning and communications at PC headquarters, I received Mr. Stanfield's blessing to take up the cudgels elsewhere. I did so, not sure of what I was getting into.

I was sad to be leaving Ottawa, especially Bob Stanfield and my friends on his staff. But the 1974 election defeat was Stanfield's third, and under the unspoken rules of the day, that was the limit. Fortunately, a real chance to make a difference, as a staffer for one of the most progressive and humane premiers in Ontario's history, beckoned. Davis was the slightly chubby, totally decent promoter of access to higher education for all, regardless of economic status. It sure seemed worth a shot.

CHAPTER 10

On the Davis Team

▼

If I have seen further,

it is by standing on the shoulders of giants.

ISAAC NEWTON

▲

THERE IS LITTLE DOUBT that what happens in Ottawa has some impact
on the lives of average Canadians. But much of what happens there is
actually more about Ottawa itself, the village of ten thousand people who
cluster around, work for, and depend upon the federal government and
Parliament for their livelihoods. This is true of most capitals, although
the artificiality of Ottawa as a federal capital accentuates the self-
reverential difference.

What happens in Ottawa is often about who is on top, who might
soon be on top, who deserves to be on top, and who can be knocked off
whatever perch he or she holds at the moment, typically by the media.
The same is true for the deputy ministers who are shuffled, the ambas-
sadors and high commissioners who are appointed by the government
du jour, the foreign diplomats who are sent to Ottawa, and the myriad of
trade organizations, think-tanks, and lobby and legal firms who seek to
influence policy in the interests of their clients, members, or agendas,
noble or otherwise.

None of this is evil or inappropriate. On occasion, evidence of impropri-
ety will emerge, whether substantial or concocted. By and large, though,

Ottawa functions as a series of competitions, big and small, over what should be on the national fiscal or policy agenda, what rank those items should have, and who should get to decide. There are tussles, not only among political parties, regional interests, and competing cabinet ministers, but also between departments over who will "hold the pen" on the final draft of a policy, regulation, or initiative. Issues such as taxation, block and grant funding to the provinces, university research, defence, national security, and foreign relations are central to Ottawa's mission and to the federal jurisdiction. But the granular effect of those mega-themes on the lives of Canadians is at best modest and at worst marginal.

In the mid-1990s, when Finance Minister Paul Martin slashed federal spending, what he really did was slash Ottawa's transfer payments vital to the provinces' section 92 obligations, including social programs. These cuts, which reduced transfers by a full third, shaved billions of dollars from the health, education, and welfare budgets of every Canadian province. How that translated into street-level reality for patients, university students, and the poor was a decision left for each provincial government to hassle with in legislatures, cabinet rooms, and inter-departmental committees. The decision to diminish transfers was not grounded in indifference to the prospects of average Canadians, as Opposition parties with strong bases in the regions loved to allege. It was about the difference between federal and provincial powers, as set out in sections 91 and 92 of the Constitution and the British North America Act.

Unlike their federal counterparts, the areas that come under provincial jurisdiction – schools, hospitals, municipalities, local environmental regulation, highways, welfare, post-secondary education, housing, and local policing – intimately touch the daily lives of most Canadians. As a result, issues such as rent control, zoning laws, aid for the disadvantaged, school class size, the training and hiring of teachers, the way that doctors are paid, contracts for nurses and other key health providers, the strength of fire departments, labour laws and practices, food prices, consumer rights, and the entire field of commercial regulation constantly wash up in provincial media. These issues become grist for the debates and controversies at Queen's Park and in the other provincial legislatures across Canada.

There is a difference in both intensity and immediacy between a federal debate about changes to the Canada Health Act and a debate involving the Ontario legislature and the Ontario Medical Association on what the compensation rates should be for doctors in the next Ontario health insurance contract. There is a similar difference between a broad debate in Ottawa about possible changes to the Criminal Code and provincial negotiations about how municipal and provincial police forces should be trained to deal with family violence or mental illness. Provincial media coverage is different too, offering more opportunity for dramatic human interest stories and in-depth journalism. For example, the *Toronto Star* ran articles about poverty-stricken older single women who had to choose between paying their rent or buying food. After the 1975 Ontario election, these stories helped put the legislature on the spot, pressure that ultimately led to the guaranteed annual income supplement for seniors.

Before I moved to Toronto, I had some sense of how Queen's Park influenced people's lives. My understanding had been acquired mostly through my experience as the student rep on the Ontario Student Awards Advisory Committee. Our deliberations had an actual impact on how much money lower-income students received, how that money had to be paid back, and how much of it was loan as opposed to grant. If that were true for post-secondary students, I thought it must be even truer in areas such as health care, housing, and poverty abatement, which affected people in communities large and small. And from the time I began attending the campaign committee meetings, chaired by the legendary advertising guru and unabashed Tory partisan Norman Atkins, I was impressed by the extent to which local issues that defied any meaning-ful right or left political rhetoric dominated campaign calculations. The building of this or that road; the location of this or that school or liquor store; the wing of this hospital in riding A versus the wing of another hospital in riding B; the state of the ambulance service in a certain rural area; the granting of a permit for the gravel pit the next seat over: all these things developed a measure of importance in an electoral map that was generally influenced by three-way splits among Tories, Liberals, and New Democrats.

It was clear that, unlike in federal politics, the reputation of the local provincial incumbent or candidate was of far more importance than swings or trends. Keeping a reasonably popular incumbent on the team was almost always the best choice. This differed federally, where the party leader and the party label meant far more.

In Ontario, Premier Davis's commanding victory in 1971 had been the triumph of the federal organizers and campaign people who were loaned to him after he won the leadership convention that year. I had become a member of "Youth for Davis" because Davis had impressed me as minister of university affairs and because of his deep commitment to post-secondary education access for all qualified students.

In 1971, the combined work of a moderate Republican pollster named Robert Teeter and an assembled "best of all talents" advertising and communications group had led to an innovative province-wide Tory campaign. The plan was based on core party principles and platform commitments, using the local and province-wide polling. It produced an integrated, uniform, and consistent tour, speech content, advertising, and policy approach for the first time in Ontario politics. The media dubbed this the "Big Blue Machine." Its success was celebrated in some quarters and attacked in others. The old approach, in which the leader said what he said, when local candidates had their own campaign priorities and made their own promises, where signs looked different from riding to riding, and advertising and tours were uncoordinated, had given ward captains and regional chieftains more power. They were the ones who controlled the message and thereby controlled the riding and the candidate. So the usual voices that favoured local say-and-sway were not excited by these thematically integrated efforts.

But the success of 1971 could not be trifled with. That election was not only a new page in modern Progressive Conservative politics but the beginning of more organized politics for Conservative politicians right across the country. Subsequently, the campaign for Ontario's October 1975 election had some snakes-and-ladders ups and downs that were both memorable and deeply instructive. The relative slide in the polls that the Davis government had experienced since the previous election had a circus-like quality that, on reflection, was a potent symbol of what politics would become in an ever-more interconnected age. American media influence into scandals large and small was infiltrating the Canadian political landscape. Richard Nixon's Watergate problems had created a media itch to find similar examples of corruption in Canada.

Although the alleged misdoings in this country never really measured up, a sort of "scandal envy" mindset had been put in motion by a determined chunk of the media.

During the 1972–74 reign of Trudeau's minority government, Tories and New Democrats conspired to force the Liberals into creating Canada's first campaign donation disclosure and expenditure rules. This effort was led by Ron Atkey, Tory MP for St. Paul's in Toronto, a well-rounded legal scholar and corporate lawyer of genuine standing.

The contagion rule in politics – namely, that even if something in another jurisdiction has no bearing on your own, some journalist or politician will insist that it does – was very much at work. So, in response to the federal rules on campaign expenditures, the Davis government established a Commission on Election Contributions and Expenses under Dalton Camp and Doug Fisher. These two estimable journalists steered a rational and overdue course to tighter controls on what could be spent, how much had to be disclosed, and who could and could not donate to election campaigns in Ontario. Their work was informed by their experience. Camp was a communications wizard for successful Tory campaigns in Nova Scotia, New Brunswick, Ontario, and Manitoba, and had run himself in Don Valley in 1968 for Robert Stanfield. Fisher, an NDP MP from Thunder Bay, had beaten the allegedly invincible Liberal minister of everything, C.D. Howe, to win the seat. That both men were respected columnists, Camp from the leftish centre right and Fisher from the rightish centre left, made their partnership even more persuasive. Their commission's fearless recommendations forever changed the rules on our country's campaign financing. It is one of the reasons that Canada takes a properly regulated route, unlike the United States, where politics is defined by a rolling-in-cash money-fest.

Even so, the four years since 1971 had found the Ontario Tories too often in retreat against the pro-people, pro-social-justice advocacy of Stephen Lewis, the articulate and passionate NDP leader. The Ontario Liberals, largely a small-town, right-wing rump with urban seats in francophone and first-generation immigrant ridings, objected to "too much change," which became their clarion call. They opposed the Davis government's reorganization of municipal scope via the creation of regional governments, such as the one that established Metro Toronto from the previously separate fiefdoms of Scarborough, North York, East York,

Swansea, Forest Hill, etc. The reorganization meant a more rational tax base, where all who shared the economic and service benefits of an integrated region also shared the tax burden for services such as police and transport. But the move gored a lot of small-time oxen who did not wish to give up the imperious municipal posts that they often won by acclamation or with less than 30 percent of the electorate showing up to vote. The opposition was challenging for the government in many ridings.

Watching this play out from the most junior position on Davis's campaign committee was a revelation. The 1975 election taught me several very important lessons about the politics of change, especially in the complex, growing, and sophisticated multi-level political culture of Ontario.

First, contagion matters. When John Napier Turner, a popular and persuasive finance minister, resigned from the Trudeau cabinet just before the 1975 provincial election, it contributed to a sense of Liberal dysfunction and arrogance. This helped the Ontario Tories overcome the Liberal lead in the polls to hang on to office. Logic? Zero.

Second, Ontarians dislike seeing too much power in the hands of a single organization. After campaigning against the price and wage freeze proposed by Robert Stanfield in the 1974 election, Trudeau put controls into place less than a year later, under a body called the Anti-Inflation Board. This board enraged Ontario Liberal voters, and Trudeau's about-face encouraged many Ontarians who did not want to vote for Mr. Davis to support the NDP instead. This made Stephen Lewis, the popular leader of the Opposition, a very serious political threat to the Tories. Lewis faced a fifty-one-seat Bill Davis minority government after the 1975 election.

Third, social justice matters in provincial politics. The 1974 federal election, in which the PC Party was hit hard by our nation-wide position on a ninety-day price and wage freeze, had convinced me that the Liberal victory was fuelled by resistance to change. I concluded that most voters desired continuity rather than change – even change that was driven by social-justice concerns. Federal Liberals were the default choice when it came to management skills and the modulated aspirations of the Canadian political centre. Not too hot and not too cold. The 1975 Ontario election showed me how wrong I was. When the *Toronto Star*, to its credit, underscored stories of what high and rising rents were doing to fixed-income seniors and others, rent control and its necessity became a core thematic in the provincial campaign. Under Davis's prodding and leadership, the Tories ended up on the side of rent control – a place the NDP had always been. In the NDP's case, this stance was part of a coherent ideology, regarding which the party was unapologetic. By contrast, Premier Davis saw rent control as an unavoidable necessity to stem an imbalance in the housing market that should be moderated, at least for a time. I remember discussions about what the lack of rent control was doing to lower-income working-class Ontarians and how that reality affected Davis's view. The Liberals, deeply in hock to developers and landlords, could not get there. The election result? Tories on top, with a minority government. The NDP in second place and the Liberals in third had an almost equal number of seats in the legislature.

Fourth, splitting the Opposition votes is the best way to win in Ontario. In 1975, very marginal changes to the three-way split in the province and tiny seat-by-seat shifts made all the difference. In Ontario, politics is a war, not of miles or yards, but of inches. Local issues really matter, and translating "regard for your leader" into voter intention is about as serious a mission as there is in provincial politics.

Fifth, arrogance always hurts. In a TV debate that became famous, Davis called the moderator, the popular and trusted CFTO news host Fraser Kelly, "Mr. Fraser." This stumble was noted. The Liberal leader, Robert Nixon from Brant County (son of the last Liberal premier of Ontario), had arrogantly misrepresented and purposely distorted Davis's record in the lead-up to the debate. Davis was visibly uncomfortable, having to hit hard at Nixon for this. Nixon's arrogance hurt the Liberal cause, but Davis's performance did galvanize the somewhat flaccid Tory vote. However, most importantly, the debate introduced disaffected Liberal voters to Stephen Lewis, whose articulate, precise, and good-humoured performance contrasted sharply with Nixon's. Lewis's sincere championing of the disadvantaged helped as well. Davis looked as if he were fighting for his political life. Lewis was campaigning for all those outside the charmed circle of prosperity that the Davis government had helped expand. Nixon, for his part, looked like a politician who was ahead in the polls, complacent in his assumed victory. Nor was he aided by being in the same party as Pierre Trudeau. His decision to side with developers against rent control was probably central to Davis winning a minority government. My lesson from that? It's both morally wrong and politically narrow to ignore those in need.

And sixth, local volunteers matter. Ross De Geer, executive director of the Ontario PC Party, and youth campaign chairs John Tory and Michael Daniher in the inner-city ridings ran a forceful "get-out-the-vote" operation. In tandem with calibrated provincially themed and locally nuanced ads, it ultimately translated into a Tory victory, however marginal.

At the 1975 election night celebrations in Brampton, Premier Davis's home seat, Tories seemed remarkably demoralized at not having received a majority. I was deeply puzzled by their discouragement. I remember saying to Kathleen Davis, the premier's bright, affable, and even-handed wife, "Where I come from, Mrs. Davis, in federal Tory politics, this looks pretty good – pretty good to me!" Her warm smile was more about a kindhearted response to my youthful enthusiasm than about agreement.

▼

Since I was the only member of the campaign team who had worked in minority government, as Robert Stanfield's legislative assistant between 1972 and 1974, I was chosen to take on the same role in the premier's office after the 1975 election. The joy of working with Ed Stewart, then the non-partisan cabinet secretary, and other members of the Davis team was almost too much to bear. Here I was, a cab driver's son from Montreal, at the day-to-day survival centre of a minority Progressive Conservative government, led by a thoroughly decent and humane Red Tory. *Incroyable!*

In 1975, the Opposition parties, who held a majority on the Standing Committee on Social Development, voted to reduce the salaries of Minister of Social Development Margaret Birch and her deputy minister to one dollar annually for their lack of action on seniors' poverty. At that point, I discovered just how decent and socially engaged my co-workers were.

After the committee vote, the deputy minister came to see me. "What are we going to do about the salary cut?" he asked. I explained patiently that a committee report is not law unless and until it is approved by the legislature. But more importantly, the Opposition parties would certainly not be forcing an election over his and his minister's salary.

I wondered exactly how serious the other parties were about the seniors' poverty issue, since, aside from the rent control connection, it had not come up during the recent election campaign.

I spoke with W. Darcy McKeough, a powerful politician from Chatham-Kent and a favourite on Bay Street and in the rank and file. He led the Treasury, Economics and Intergovernmental Affairs (Finance) Ministry. After the discussion and vote relating to the salary cut for the minister and deputies, he ordered his ministry and the Social Development Ministry to undertake an in-depth review of seniors' poverty. What they found was troubling. Thirty-five percent of Ontarians over sixty-five (most of them women) were living below the poverty line. Stories about buying dog and cat food to "beef up" low-income diets were not apocryphal. This study brought action. Within weeks, the guaranteed annual income supplement for seniors was passed into law. The poverty rate for the over-sixty-fives collapsed to less than 5 percent within twenty-four months. My modest role in helping this along as a legislative negotiator was one of the most satisfying collaborations I could ever have hoped for. And the risk of a de facto confidence vote over the minister and deputy minister's salaries, which the government might well have lost, thus forcing another election, had abated.

Ontario became the first Canadian province to go this anti-poverty route. That the approach spread to other provinces, and was finally incorporated in the federal guaranteed income supplement, shows that, with the interaction of the major parties, solid journalistic coverage, and public service determination, a minority government can build something constructive.

In my life-long engagement on the road to a better approach to poverty, this would be a turning point of deep and everlasting impact.

CHAPTER 11

From Public to Private and Back

▼

The most practical kind of politics

is the politics of decency.

THEODORE ROOSEVELT

▲

IN MY FIRST BOOK, *No Surrender,* I referred to the next period of my life as "time served in the Brampton Legions." Lying just to the northwest of Mississauga, Brampton was Premier William Davis's riding. In working for Davis and seeing his deep relationship with his riding, from its early history as the rural county of Peel to its slow development into a multi-racial, multicultural urban community, I developed a sensitivity for, and an affinity with, the way that Ontario itself was changing. This largely Protestant farm area transformed in a relatively short time into a deeply urbanized area where Indo-Canadians and Asian Canadian populations built on a base that had already been increased by massive immigration from southern Europe, especially Italy, Greece, and Portugal. The building and expansion of primary and secondary schools, colleges, roads, sewer systems, and hospitals; the increase in Sunday Masses at Brampton's single Catholic church, on Main Street; and the construction of new mosques, temples, and community centres were all symbolic of the province's transformation. The Bill Davis government saw accommodation and bridge building as central to shaping a society with the decency and capacity to encourage growth while simultaneously protecting both diversity and economic opportunity.

In 1975, Ontarians had chosen a centre-left legislature. Whatever successes and failures the Davis government had produced during the years between 1971 and 1975, this new verdict was unavoidable and could not be ignored. A minority government gives everyone a chance to learn about balance, measure, engagement, and how progress is really achieved. Whether on economic and social issues, the Constitution, or French-language rights, no democratic politician can allow herself or himself the luxury of forging ahead, come what may. In a minority parliament, you must put some water in your wine.

Bob Rae, reflecting on his time as Ontario's sole NDP premier and on his later role as a Liberal, often says that it is not enough for leaders to be moral, humane, progressive, or principled. They also need the ability, the reach, and the networks to convince people that, on specific issues, they are right. Many CCF/NDP leaders who believed in social progress and fairness didn't manage to convince enough people to vote for their party. As Rae would say, "It is not good enough to stand for the right things, fight for the noble and uplifting, if one does not figure out how to bring the public along. Leadership is also about persuasion, at least in a democracy."

My front row seat in the 1975 election and beyond for the movement on education policies and teachers' right to strike, the patriation of the Constitution, the negotiation of the Charter of Rights and Freedoms, the decision to not expand the Spadina Expressway, the public support of Crown endeavours in urban transit, the support for de Havilland aircraft, the establishment of NorOntair, and the expansion of TVOntario taught me a core premise of successful politics in Canada's most populous province: why you want to achieve change is important. How you attempt to do it matters even more. The bear trap of majority governments is the illusion of power they create. When one party has enough seats in the legislature to pass any bill it chooses, compromise, listening, adjusting, and even constructive delay – yes, that is a real term in government decision making – can be seen as a sign of weakness or lack of will, especially by its own partisans. As Pierre Trudeau found out with everything from the Carter White Paper on Taxation ("a buck is a buck") to the National Energy Program some years later, and even with the War Measures Act, concluding that you are absolutely right and that listening to others will produce less than optimum results in terms of public policy, not to mention your own political prospects, always comes at a cost. There is a very fine line between strong-willed, decisive government and arrogance. The former is usually overstated in terms of value, the latter almost always corrosive to political credibility.

Serving as legislative secretary to the premier gave me the opportunity to witness, and sometimes advise on, the ways in which a minority government plays out. New structures were put in place through which to work beneficially with the Opposition parties. A new Legislative Planning Committee was struck to bring my counterparts in the other parties and the respective House leaders into the planning cycle. I collaborated with colleagues on all sides in good faith, as they did with me. Our motto was akin to the marketing slogan of the Holiday Inn at the time: "No surprises."

Each party had a rationale for maintaining stability, at least for a year or two. They needed time to consolidate and raise money. They wanted to use the legislature to plant their flag on issues, without punching a hole in the boat and causing an election. A minority government meant that some suggestions and ideas from the other parties had to be given serious consideration for inclusion in government laws and programs. If Ontarians had wanted one party to hold all the cards, or even most of them, they would have said so on election day. They had said quite the opposite.

The election results also meant that the Davis government needed to reach out to Ontarians who had felt excluded from the allegedly Toronto-centric decisions made between 1971 and 1975. Labour and agricultural economists were appointed to bodies such as the Ontario Economic Council. The Ontario Business Advocacy Council was created as a forum through which small business could engage with the Province. The premier met regularly with the head of the Ontario Federation of Labour, Cliff Pilkey, who hailed from Durham County. There is an old Rumi proverb from Persia: "The grass grows with rain, not thunder." The Brampton version of this, as expressed by Bill Davis, was, "You know, Hughie, you catch more flies with honey than with vinegar."

Those days of minority government taught me not only what our sovereigntist friends in Quebec called *étapisme* (the tactic of step-by-step progress) but the importance of working with people who understood that approach. Three individuals – Ed Stewart, Clare Westcott, and Bob Elgie – come to mind here. They all understood étapisme.

Ed Stewart, the government's clerk of the cabinet, came from Windsor. He had served as deputy minister when Davis was minister of university affairs, and when Davis became premier, he made Ed cabinet secretary within the first year. Ed's dad, who worked in what was then the Ford plant in Windsor, was a shop steward for the United Automobile Workers (now UNIFOR). In September 1975, my first week on the job, Ed invited me to join him at a meeting where twenty-five-year service pins were being awarded to a large group of Ontario public servants. As we walked back to the Legislative Building afterward, Ed said something I have never forgotten: "There were a group of people in that room with a collective history of hundreds of years of service in Ontario, in many departments and regions. Any morning you wake up and decide that you know more than they do on an issue of complexity, give your head a shake. They are not right on everything. No one ever is. But they are rarely totally wrong on anything." My respect for the Ontario civil service remained undiminished from that moment.

Clare Westcott, the premier's executive assistant, understood that offering a helping hand to people in need was as much a part of Davis's remit, if not more so, as negotiating with Ottawa or meeting with investment bankers in New York, London, or Frankfurt. I would meet with Clare on an issue that was important to an MPP, whether on our side or on the other side of the legislature. I always arrived a half hour early so that when Clare waved me into his office, I could listen to him work the phones, offering help to Ontarians: he might support a constituent who was having trouble getting a nursing home bed for a relative, or arrange seats at a Maple Leafs' game for a group of orphans, or follow up on a letter from someone who had been denied access to Ontario Housing.

Bob Elgie, elected in 1977, with a background in both the law and neurosurgery, brought in a new Human Rights Code to protect the LGBT community. Ontario's PC government was engaged with, and often fighting for, those on the margins. A seniors' property tax credit was established to help keep seniors of modest means in their homes and living independently as long as possible.

Stewart, Westcott, and Elgie, as well as other remarkable Tories, shared a strong bias in terms of reaching out, inclusion, and addressing the gaps in opportunity and advantage that plague modern Ontario society and the country as a whole. Their conservatism was progressive, their concern about the disadvantaged was genuine and palpable. They had a signal impact on my view of what government should, at its best, be about. This was not so much about Red versus Blue Tories – these are simplistic typologies that impart little of value. It was about government as an agent of balance and fairness, always looking for more ways to increase equality of opportunity while sustaining productive and economically vibrant societies.

Throughout this period, my personal life changed dramatically for the better. I met, courted, and married Donna Armstrong of Kingston, Ontario, a Queen's graduate in nursing science. I had never met anyone with her mix of beauty, intellectual breadth, solid judgment, and immense good humour. Her welcoming family was French Canadian from La Mauricie (Shawinigan) in Quebec on her mother's side and Scottish-Anglo from Woodstock and St. Andrews, New Brunswick, on her father's side. Their background could not have been more different from mine. Our Anglo, Scottish, French Canadian, Jewish union was wonderfully championed by Donna's mom, Jacqueline, a Cossette from Shawinigan. Her love, loyalty, and deep maternal instincts revealed a depth of character and decency that are rare and sorely needed in the world. The Cossettes were a working-class family: Donna's uncle Georges and grandfather Hormidas had been a foremen in the Belgo mill in Shawinigan and were part of the hard-working, decent people who lived in the lower town (bas-ville) area of the community. The Anglo managers lived up the hill.

After the 1977 election, in which Davis won a second and stronger minority government, I spoke one day with Eddie Goodman, a senior lawyer in Toronto and long-time grandee of federal and provincial Conservative politics. "In life, you can't stay forever on one narrow path," Eddie pointed out. "You don't have any business experience, Hughie, and business is a huge part of how healthy societies generate wealth, growth, and jobs. You're a married man now. Maybe it's time to leave this comfortable post and make your way in the business world?"

When we moved to London, Ontario, I followed Eddie's advice. Donna's career took us there. It was in health care, and she had been accepted to pursue her MBA studies at Western University. In London, I was hired as the director of corporate and investor relations at the headquarters of John Labatt, the holding company that owned Labatt Breweries, Ault Dairies, Laura Secord Candies, Ogilvie Mills, Inniskillin Wines, and a host of other food-industry-related companies, as well as the Toronto Blue Jays. I enjoyed my time there very much, especially the challenge of working for a dynamic Canadian company, heavily unionized with differing shareholder, stakeholder, and customer interests. Public and regulatory policy, community and philanthropic support, and financial market relations were all part of my remit. I knew that in most Canadian provinces, the brewing industry paid the highest of industrial wages. Seeing that Labatt treated its employees with respect and care, invested heavily in community charities and organizations, and engaged with government was a remarkable education for me. My portfolio covered items as diverse as the Ontario Milk Marketing Board, whether the US State Department would react negatively when the Blue Jays hired Cuban ball players (it would), regulated beer prices, and the use by Canadian vintners of the term "champagne" – and that was just one week's work! Coming to understand the nuances of financial markets and the broad grid of relationships between large public companies and local, national, and provincial governments was also a valuable experience. And being responsible for the company's overall approach to charitable donations across Canada brought me into contact with many of the not-for-profit and social capital organizations that fill the gaps neither government nor the pure operations of the market economy can address.

In 1979, however, I was asked back to Queen's Park because energy negotiations were looming with what would be the short-run federal government of Joe Clark. The Davis government had serious disagreements with Ottawa over taxation and energy. I attended the 1979 provincial premiers' meeting in Pointe-au-Pic, Quebec, as an advisor to the premier. (While in the private sector, I had been made vice-chair of the Ontario Advisory Committee on Confederation, created after the election of René Lévesque in 1976.) There was a strong divide at this meeting between Alberta premier Peter Lougheed's view that everyone should pay the same price for Alberta crude and Premier Davis's view that there should be both a world price and a more reasonable price for Canadian consumers. After all, since the time of the Diefenbaker government, the latter had paid higher prices to help finance exploration and production in Alberta, or at least consumers in Ontario had. Imposing a world price on Canadian oil would increase the cost-of-living burden on the many people in rural and small-town Ontario who had no choice but to drive older pickup trucks and cars because public transit was unavailable to them.

In the years leading up to 1982, Bill Davis was a strong advocate of Prime Minister Trudeau's proposed patriation of the Constitution. In doing so, he reached across the political spectrum to support the national leader of a rival party despite opposition from eight premiers and factions of our own federal and provincial Tory caucus. The stakes were high in negotiations. They were about protecting the rights and freedoms of immigrants, many of whom had left their countries in hopes of finding greater freedoms in Canada. They were about language guarantees for English-speaking minorities in Quebec and French-speaking minorities elsewhere. And they were about beginning the constitutional recognition of the inherent rights of Indigenous populations, which had been left out of the constitutional family for so long. The battle was not easy for Davis, but it was a vital one, more important to him than winning the next election. Those of us who were fortunate enough to see his level of engagement up close understood that it was about his commitment to national fairness and the equilibrium vital for the survival and success of Canada. His typification of the Charter of Rights and Freedoms was not about right or left, or preferring the written proscriptive approach to constitutions in the non-Anglo world to the Parliament-is-supreme perspective of the Anglosphere. It was about protecting average people from government: from unfair search and seizure, and from the tyranny of the majority – tyrannies exemplified by the lead-up to the Second World War and stirred up by our own War Measures Act in 1970. It was about recognizing that the vast majority of people who get into trouble with the police, or who become the guests of Her Majesty in our prisons, are from the 15 percent of the population who live beneath the poverty line.

I had the privilege of participating in the patriation negotiations as Ontario's associate secretary of cabinet for federal-provincial affairs. In the end, I felt that progress had been made toward recognition of First Nations rights to self-government and equal rights for women. Totally absent from the talks, however, was any reference to the link between unprotected rights and low economic prospects. Our prisons, as I mention above, had, and still have, a disproportionate representation of poor Canadians, and the First Nation population is also wildly over-represented. The fact that the ranks of the poor disproportionately include women, people of colour, First Nations brothers and sisters, and recent immigrants amplifies the divisive role that poverty plays.

Our daughter, Jacqueline Sadye Armstrong Segal, was born in 1982. My late mom never met her. My mother-in-law, Jacqueline Armstrong, doted on her granddaughter Jacqueline for many wonderful years. With Jacqueline's birth, I concluded it was time to leave the vicissitudes of politics and move back to the private sector. By the fall of 1982, after sorting through offers from banking, insurance, and the civil service, I had decided on advertising and marketing. My new boss was my long-time friend Norman Atkins. He and I had been through the 1975, 1977, and 1981 elections together, not only on the same side but also working closely. Norman was not a policy wonk, but his political antennae were astoundingly well tuned to reality on the street and the nuance of public opinion. His belief in Bill Davis was deep and abiding. His loyalty to Robert Stanfield was legendary in Tory political circles. His work for Richard Hatfield in New Brunswick was one of the keys to Hatfield's success.

Norman felt that moderation was the secret to success for Progressive Conservatives, federally and provincially. He detested the ideological self-indulgence of the party's right wing, who embraced the TINA (There Is No Alternative) approach associated with Margaret Thatcher's time in office. My take was that, from everything I had seen in provincial and federal politics so far, success was about more than just moderation. It was about coherent strategies and initiatives to ensure that the economic mainstream continued to widen. Generally speaking, people with inherited wealth or firm financial prospects, or those who had worked hard to get a leg up in terms of education, housing, health, and positive outcomes, did not need government support. They needed an economic frame and a balance of tax, venture, and opportunity policies that encouraged their investment and diligence. The real challenge was to

change things for those who lived outside this magic circle and who
were having great difficulty reaching or staying above the poverty line.

Almost every governing instrument that I saw deployed or debated
during the Davis years, though laudable, had relied on moderation. They
included financial assistance to post-secondary students and the guaranteed income supplement for poor seniors, as well as the family law
reforms instigated by Attorney General Roy McMurtry that sought to
ensure equal economic rights for women in separation or divorce. And
the minister of women's issues, Robert Welch, had launched an anti-
family-violence initiative. In the violence initiative, the challenge and the
purpose of the campaign were clear – to inform women that they could
call a 1-800 number and get out from under the abuse. In many cases,
though, they hesitated to leave, because they were financially dependent
on their abuser. Through the solicitor general's department, Attorney
General McMurtry had produced a memorandum of enforcement, under
which any police report of family violence should see the woman and
children made safe and the husband or partner detained pending inves-
tigation. Other programs, including investment in inner-city schools,
the creation of family health clinics, and nutrition and exercise courses,
were about reaching the children of folks who lived near or beneath the
poverty line.

But they didn't deal with poverty itself. I believed that until the Tories
showed courage and tackled the issue directly, the real enemies of social
cohesion, the myriad pathologies associated with poverty – poor health
outcomes, problems with the police, substance abuse, family breakup,
and poor educational performance for kids – would continue unabated.
And the gap between rich and poor would simply become more glaring
every day. I had reminded McMurtry that Robert Stanfield had championed a guaranteed annual income prior to and at the Niagara conference in 1969 and of our discussions earlier that year at Little Whitefish
Lake, but he needed no reminder. Every day in his role as attorney general, McMurtry focused on the justice system as a proxy for fairness
overall.

My nine years in the private sector brought me into contact with a
wide variety of advertising clients. I came to see that brand equity, the
reputation of a product, company, or service, was about more than just

advertising or price. It was about reputation – a reputation that said to consumers that a company could be trusted, that its profit-making mission was not devoid of social responsibility or product integrity. From airlines to financial concerns, from beer to courier services, from mining to entertainment to hospitality, what your company stood for and what you were offering people and the larger community always mattered. Shortcuts to raise profits always came up short. Companies produce products, services, and intellectual value added, and they work with their own management and employees to do so effectively and profitably. They are measured quarterly by profits, by gross revenues, and by how well they manage costs. Shareholders have every right to expect meaningful measures of success or precise explanations of why success might be put off. Governments are also about outcomes – but outcomes that become the foundations upon which citizens, companies, volunteer groups, communities, and organizations of all kinds construct their own futures because the foundations are fair, sustainable, humane, and well built.

What I learned about the intersection of private and public enterprise was invaluable to determining how I viewed the nuances of a mixed-market economy. My involvement in organizations such as the Atlantic Council, the Canadian Institute of Strategic Studies, and the Conference Board added a rare opportunity to understand the middle ground between the private sector and the public policy world. That, plus my continued volunteer work in various election campaigns for Progressive Conservative or moderate centrist candidates across the country, made the decade between 1982 and 1991 comparable to an advanced practical master's degree in the political and economic linkages that shaped the reality of Canadian society. At close quarters, I was able to study the workings of a modern and competitive society, with its many products and services, political ideas and platforms, and competing views on priorities by those seeking to influence the public agenda. My youthful fealty to Progressive Conservative centre-right politics evolved into a more precise appreciation that partisan preference and competition, though important to any democracy, were not the sum total of what mattered. The views of those who were not partisan also counted. I learned this lesson through hundreds of interactions with marketers, financiers, regulators, product designers, entrepreneurs, customers, union leaders, employees, and others who made the non-political world run. I also recognized that those in the trade union movement, who were proponents of social change more radical than many governments could embrace, deserved to be treated fairly. Like the hard-hearted, far-right, laissez-faire, survival-of-the-fittest Blue Tories, they were sometimes shrill, but they added important balance to the debate – and were not infrequently right.

Throughout that time, my views on the alleviation of poverty remained firm. As I pursued my private-sector career, I felt certain that, though government could do many things around the edges, failing to address the poverty issue head-on was a central and serious error that would eventually erode the legitimacy of government itself. This was not about a road or path that might helpfully be taken. It was about a challenge that, if ignored, would become the soft underbelly of the demonstrable achievements of both capitalism and free markets, on the one hand, and the liberal-democratic world order, on the other. What my decade in the private sector brought home in real day-to-day terms was that one aspect of the market-driven underpinning of much of our economy is both correct and central to how society should work. When a business knows that it has a core product defect, or organizational misfire, or flawed marketing stance, the only right course of action is to deal with it straight up. We know that poverty and all of its pathologies produce increased health care costs, lousy educational attainment, difficulties with the law, family tensions, substance abuse, and a myriad of other socially unhelpful and economically expensive outcomes. Failing to deal with it directly, as we have with seniors' poverty, is simply avoiding a central threat to our social cohesion and economic productivity as a province, nation, or free world. I was convinced of this in 1982, and I remain even more so today.

CHAPTER 12

Learning from Mulroney

▼

The only thing that saves us
from the bureaucracy is its inefficiency.

SENATOR EUGENE McCARTHY

▲

IN 1980, DURING MY TIME as Bill Davis's associate cabinet secretary for federal-provincial affairs, I travelled with the premier to Quebec, where the Parti Québécois had called a referendum on sovereignty for the province. Davis was a soldier for the "no" side of separation. Two shining stars of Quebec's legal and business communities, Brian Mulroney and Paul Martin, were also firmly on the federalist side. Mulroney had made a bid to become leader of the Progressive Conservative Party in 1976, and many of the organizers from his failed attempt were principal voices of the federalist "no" campaign.

During the 1976 leadership convention, I had supported neither Mulroney nor the eventual winner, Joe Clark. I chose instead to support the Quebec francophone candidate, Claude Wagner. His plans on foreign policy and defence were conservative, but on social policy and income security he was more progressive and tempered than the other candidates.

I had known Mulroney from earlier days, when his volunteer activism for leaders such as Robert Stanfield was at the centre of any hope our party might have in Quebec. He was always hard working and engaged. No one was better than Mulroney at working a room with good humour and genuine recognition of others. His ambition for self-advancement was evident (and when isn't it, where politics, business, or academe are involved?), but he maintained a strong link to his humble background on Quebec's north shore, his dad's working-class roots as an electrician, and the idea of small-town folks, with larger world hopes and aspirations. If an issue of the heart were involved – poverty, suffering, intrinsic unfairness – Mulroney's instincts were always to help, sometimes to his detriment. He took another run at the PC leadership in 1983, this time successfully, and two months later won a by-election in Central Nova, Nova Scotia, to become the MP representing that riding. From then on, Mulroney had my unwavering support, even as my career in the private sector and as a Skelton-Clark fellow at the School of Policy Studies at Queen's University continued.

Working with Mulroney as a volunteer in his 1984 and 1988 federal election campaigns, then afterward in 1991 as a senior policy advisor and ultimately his chief of staff, would encompass almost a decade of my life. Sometimes my role was minor, other times all-consuming. But at all times, no one ever had to wonder what might be on Brian Mulroney's mind. He had two of the most vital characteristics of inspired, effective leadership. First, a genuine ambition to win, with the willingness to put in the necessary hard work. Second, an understanding of why he wanted to win. That meant knowing what he wanted to do if he were elected to govern.

As prime minister, Mulroney would not succeed everywhere. But his passion to advance free trade, conciliation with Quebec, land claims progress for First Nations, environmental innovation, tax reform, new infrastructure, and a reformed family allowance to increase support for low-income families with children left Canada a stronger, more inclusive place. Since Confederation, governments had promised to build a bridge to Prince Edward Island. Mulroney found a way to get it done, just as he found a new way forward on energy price regulation between East and West, offshore resources, and actually procuring more ships for the navy and other kit for national defence.

Despite counter-pressures from British prime minister Margaret Thatcher and American president Ronald Reagan, Canada took a strong leadership role against apartheid in South Africa; Nelson Mandela came to Ottawa just four months after his release from prison to thank

Canadians. Mulroney's government supported the Dayton Peace Accords in the former Yugoslavia with a robust military deployment and backed the NATO stance that helped unwind the thermonuclear threat of the Cold War without a shot being fired. Under Mulroney, Canadian Naval and Air Forces were deployed in the liberation of Kuwait during the first Gulf War. His swift response to send a major Canadian food airlift to the Ethiopian famine and to appoint David MacDonald as its coordinator and subsequently ambassador to Addis Ababa connected him with my own deeply humanitarian biases and with one of the key personalities who had helped me form those biases decades earlier. All of this came from Mulroney's principled vision of Canada standing for a certain kind of world.

After the sweeping Mulroney victory in 1984, there seemed to be a strong sense that there was something vaguely illegitimate about the Tories winning so solidly, especially on the part of Trudeauphiles in the Liberal Party, academe, and the media. They were suspicious of a leader who was so brazen as to think that, without inherited wealth, a University of Toronto degree, or civil service provenance, like that of William Lyon Mackenzie King or Lester Pearson, he might actually become prime minister through hard work, Tory values, and a big heart.

Mulroney's stance within the PC family was toward consensus, especially after he defeated Joe Clark in an open convention. He appointed Clark supporters to important party and government roles, just as he did prominent Liberal and NDP personalities to diplomatic posts. Patronage was not an unpleasant burden for him, as it was for Pierre Trudeau, who delegated the task to others, or for Stephen Harper, who as Conservative prime minister delayed making those choices for as long as he could. I think Mulroney saw the assignment of appointments, among other things, as a way of humanizing government for people from outside the Ottawa bubble.

When I set aside my business life and my Skelton-Clark fellowship at the School of Policy Studies to accept Mulroney's invitation to join his staff in 1991, I did so with an immense sense of opportunity. This was not about sacrifice. Tasks related to public policy or the public interest are about the privilege of serving. I have never said no to a request from a prime minister or a premier of any affiliation. Diefenbaker's speech of 1962 is forever rooted in my memory bank – which means that, barring illness or unexpected disaster, saying no to one's country is never the right answer.

Mulroney's request that I join his team was in many ways remarkable. I had not voted for him in either leadership race. I had worked in his campaigns after he became leader, but so had hundreds of others. The case he made to me was direct.

On a Sunday afternoon in June 1991, at his request, I joined him at 24 Sussex Drive. "Hugh," he said, "I need you for three tasks that I have to address before the next election. First, with the Parti Québécois so high in the polls and Robert Bourassa angry that the Meech Lake Accord was trashed by the old Trudeau Liberal gang in Manitoba and Newfoundland, we can lose the country if we don't put forward another, more inclusive constitutional proposal. Your background with the provinces and your work during the 1981–83 Constitution cycle would really help. Next, I need the party to hang in while we get the PQ bullet out of the gun. Your relationships with the party, high and low, young and old, east and west, would make a difference. Finally, I need you to tell me whether I should run a third time, or pack it in in the interest of the country and the party."

Well, I thought, he had me at "I need." Mulroney's courage on free trade, on apartheid, and even on the politically ruinous but economically vital GST had contributed to historically low poll numbers for his government – single digits in some polls. And he was a centrist, fighting sovereignists in Quebec and Ottawa, as well as the deeply nativist, anti-Quebec Reform insurgency in the West. When I joined his staff on August 1, 1991, the PC voter intention was at a historic low for the incumbent government.

My first assignment was to accompany Mulroney as he attended the annual general national meeting of the party at a downtown Toronto hotel. This being a Conservative meeting, there were one or two motions that delighted parts of the Tory base while simultaneously offending the Diefenbaker Bill of Rights principles. Thankfully, the resolution to disallow Sikh RCMP officers from wearing properly badged turbans as opposed to caps was handily defeated.

Most of my time during those years was taken up with the full range of chief-of-staff activities: preparing for diplomatic events, visits, and travels; participating in the numerous meetings and negotiations on the Charlottetown Accord; negotiating with my counterpart in Quebec, the trustworthy and incisive John Parisella, to keep Quebec onside; and working with other premiers' offices to maintain forward motion on various files. But remarkably, Mulroney also allowed me to chair an interdepartmental task force on a guaranteed annual income.

Eighteen months before stepping down in 1984, Pierre Trudeau appointed the Royal Commission on Economic Union and Development Prospects for Canada, chaired by Donald S. Macdonald, a former defence and finance minister and House leader in the 1968–83 Trudeau government. The Macdonald Commission was a seminal inquiry into the requirements for building prosperity and inclusion into Canada's economic future.

The commission's final report recommended that Canada enter into a free trade arrangement with the Americans, concluding that a leap of faith would yield more than could be achieved by a smaller market space and endless protectionist threats. To Macdonald's credit, the report also included a robust section on Canada's social prospects, which called for a guaranteed annual income (GAI) as an important baseline for protecting Canadian workers from employment shifts caused by global competition and competitive income costs from trading partners worldwide. The research director for that part of the commission's work was Keith Banting, a leading academic with deep and world-renowned expertise on income security challenges – the same Keith Banting who had drafted the party's first paper on the GAI, which was debated at the Niagara conference in October 1969. After John Turner's Liberal government lost the election in late 1984, the Macdonald Commission filed its report with the newly elected prime minister, Brian Mulroney.

Unfortunately, Mulroney sent the GAI recommendation to Jean de Grandpré, then CEO of Bell Canada, to review with other members of the Conseil du Patronat, a Quebec big-business lobby. Their conclusion was that the GAI was not necessary since unemployment insurance (UI) was Canada's response to job insecurity. This was, of course, a fatuous, self-serving evasion of what UI would become. Many poor Canadians had jobs, so the issue was larger than UI. As the UI program's rules were tightened and its eligibility criteria scaled up, increasing numbers of unemployed people became ineligible to receive it. A clarion chance for two-track progress on both productivity and poverty was lost quite unnecessarily.

In 1991, Benoît Bouchard, the Quebec lieutenant who replaced Lucien Bouchard, was federal minister of health and welfare. With Mulroney's support and that of Finance Minister Don Mazankowski, Bouchard had advanced a reform to replace the universal family allowance with a far more generous refundable child tax benefit that would truly help low-income children at risk. I was anxious about moving away from universality, but the fact was that for those living in poverty, the family allowance was not enough. For those who didn't need it, the reform made little difference. Mulroney and Bouchard agreed to my suggestion for a task force on moving to a guaranteed annual income tax credit (an anti-poverty tax credit), also refundable, as an appropriate next step.

When I petitioned the prime minister for this task force on a guaranteed annual income (as an allowance or a tax credit), my argument was precise. If we were changing our approach to poor families with children in favour of generosity, what about other low-income people who were also in need? Mulroney was, as he often said, "un fils du Côte-Nord du Québec" (a son of the north shore of Quebec), and having a strong base in Atlantic and rural Canada, he was keen on helping working-age people who were unemployed or living on the edge of poverty. Benoît Bouchard came from a riding in the Lac Saint-Jean part of Quebec, itself no stranger to economic and extractive industry boom-and-bust cycles, with unemployment being a regular part of life.

My role as chair of the task force (a role not normally allowed for a political chief of staff) had me working with officials from Health and Welfare Canada (its deputy minister was Ian Green, a former university roommate of mine) and other ministries. Green and I were looking for a policy opening on the issue. Officials from Treasury Board and Finance, however, were awash in delaying tactics and other workarounds to ensure that never happened. Like their counterparts throughout the world, they saw preserving the spending freedoms and prerogatives of the minister of finance as their primary duty. Alleviating poverty through automatic entitlement programs such as a GAI or a negative income tax was not on their agenda: not then and not ever. The task force met several times with all the required officials, but sadly we rowed in perfect circles because "imperial" Finance did not want any such program. With the constitutional file risk so high, I reluctantly had to abandon the course on the GAI. But on land claims, natural resource revenues for the provinces and their social programs, and the GST tax credit, Mulroney was there, intensely trying to help the low-income side of the ledger. Despite genuine deficit pressures (the government balanced its operational deficit but was paying huge amounts on the inherited debt from the Trudeau government), he did not slash transfer payments to the provinces, which were so vital for education, health, and social services, as Prime Minister Jean Chrétien subsequently did.

During my time on his staff, Mulroney also fought hard to expand the Free Trade Agreement with the United States into the North American Free Trade Agreement (NAFTA) because he believed that Canada's economic viability required more assured access for Canadian goods, services, people, and capital to a broader market. The best social policy, from his perspective, lay in creating jobs here, in Mexico, and in the United States.

Indeed, economic and job growth numbers since 1992 have been impressive for Canada, as have the trade numbers for all three NAFTA partners. The wealth created, even including the lopsided contribution of Canadian energy exports, has been notable. What has been less impressive is distributional efficiency, or fairness. Trade agreements rarely deal with this aspect of domestic economic balance. That is generally not their purpose. This was one reason the Macdonald Commission had recommended a basic income/GAI as an important balancing element. Wealth creation without a distribution strategy is, at best, only half the job. At worst, it is deeply divisive. As in the private sector, developing even a superb new product that is superior to the competition simply won't work without an adequate distribution strategy.

My last formal period working in the Executive Branch in Ottawa taught me three vital things. First, Ottawa would never be the main source of real anti-poverty reform, since the urgent would always take precedence over the truly important in an unduly media-driven town. Second, "imperial" Finance would never be a force for good or for genuine poverty relief. And third, as with other constructive reforms, the impetus for anti-poverty reform would need to come from a province or several provinces. From there, it could spread across the country, as had been the case with universal health insurance in Saskatchewan during the 1960s and Ontario's guaranteed annual income supplement for seniors in the mid-1970s. The Ontario supplement in particular was a veritable model of how provincial innovation could spread and ultimately become national.

▼

I left Ottawa in April 1993. Several of Mulroney's ministers proposed that I seek the leadership of the party, and the prime minister himself generously suggested that I consider a diplomatic or civil service post. But I made the happy choice to return to the School of Policy Studies at Queen's. My wife, Donna, and I had moved from Toronto to Kingston in 1991, because this allowed me to get home to see her and our daughter, Jacqueline, more often. Also, Donna's own civil service career had taken her to the Ontario Health Insurance Plan head office in Kingston, where she played a senior role.

The School of Policy Studies was headed by Keith Banting. Yes, the very same Oxford-trained academic, with multifaceted research and teaching experience on matters of social policy and income security. Banting had become the go-to expert on the interaction among social policy instruments, federalism, and measurable economic and political outcomes, both in Canada and beyond. He had begun doing leading-edge collaborative research on the relationship between diversity, trust, income security, and the health of democracies in Western countries. He built an exciting complement of programs and faculty at Queen's, with the support and encouragement of Richardson Hall, the central administration.

The intellectual opportunity to learn from others at Queen's was immense. George Perlin, an esteemed political science scholar and professor who had plumbed the public opinion and policy tribalism of the Tory party, was down the hall in Political Studies. In the office next to me was Tom Courchene, an economist from Princeton (originally from Saskatchewan) who led the country in the understanding of fiscal federalism/equalization – the central plumbing that was fundamental to any social policy reform – and had a special interest in Canada's Indigenous policy challenges. I admired Courchene greatly, and while he and I were both living in London, I had volunteered in his 1979 election campaign to become the PC MP for the riding of London East. Bill Fox gave a wildly popular course in understanding the media landscape. He had served as a senior bureau chief for the *Toronto Star* in Ottawa and Washington, had been communications director for Prime Minister Mulroney, and had played a remarkable role in leading Canadian corporations. His course was always oversubscribed. Ron Watts, former principal at Queen's and the world's most renowned scholar on federalism, was also close by. Watts had been a senior constitutional advisor to various Canadian prime ministers, including Mulroney, during the Charlottetown Accord cycle. He and I had attended many constitutional policy meetings in Ottawa.

Banting took the university's old school of public administration and built the new School of Policy Studies, with both a professional and an academic stream. As in earlier years, his courage rarely failed him. He would grow the school from 1.5 tenure-track positions to more than 10.0, supplementing the academic stream with practitioners, appointed as fellows or adjunct professors, who taught in the graduate program. The course I would eventually teach in the spring cycle for over twenty years focused on the theory and practicality of instrument selection in government. We examined why governments chose to address issues or serve the public in various ways – sometimes creating an agency, sometimes passing a coercive or a permissive law, sometimes regulating, sometimes negotiating federal-provincial agreements – and considered how to evaluate the effectiveness of these decisions before and after implementation. I used modern case studies on foreign, domestic, provincial, municipal, and international efforts that had failed or succeeded.

Between 1993 and 2006, my presence in the school was regular and engaged. Running many classroom sessions on basic income and poverty refined my understanding of the varied design and implementation challenges associated with them.

During that time, I combined my academic work with a life on Bay Street, joining Gluskin Sheff and Associates, a respected portfolio manager, as an advisor. I was invited to sit on boards in the energy, wine, dairy, cement, and engineering industries, where I got a rare glimpse into the fiduciary and corporate roles that are central to key parts of our economy. The net impact was to make me even more intent on refocusing the way we address poverty in Canada. Ira Gluskin and Gerry Sheff were unfailingly kind and inspiring. Seeing their community-wide philanthropic engagement and the integrity of their business mission, as prudent and successful portfolio managers for individuals and institutions, was an education in itself.

From the private sector, I learned some important realities about achieving necessary change. For example, the purpose of an initiative, policy change, investment, or new corporate development must be clear at the outset. The fuzzier the intent, the less likely a positive outcome for customers, clients, employees, or shareholders. Single-purpose initiatives have a better chance of succeeding than multi-purpose ones. If they are well planned and evidence-based, they have the highest odds of success. The realities of the marketplace and of economic, social, and political conditions truly do matter. If initiatives are not based in reality, they are not likely to succeed.

In terms of poverty, these lessons showed me that focusing on its causes or the conditions that generated it, for either an individual or a community, was actually avoiding the point. Poverty itself was, and is, a contributing cause of ill health, poor education outcomes, marriage breakup, short lives, substance abuse, and problems with the law. A single-focus program to address the cash crunch that defines and shatters millions of lives would clearly be the most efficient, humane, and productive way to proceed. The many "causes of poverty," cited usually by Finance officials who are seeking to evade any specific action at all, sustain the "poverty is complex" school of thought, which is really the "do nothing" school of thought. No state, however flush with excess cash, can address all the endless lists of causes that contribute to poverty – hence, invoking that complex myriad of causes is actually the tribal call for inertia. Determining, as we have with seniors, that we will top up their income to reduce the effects of poverty, on them and on the rest of us, is the rational model.

▼

When Brian Mulroney decided to step down, and the Tory leadership opened up in 1993, Trade Minister Michael Wilson, Defence Minister Bill McKnight, Minister for Sport Otto Jelinek, and Immigration Minister Bernard Valcourt pressured me to seek the leadership. They advanced this unlikely prospect by suggesting that Kim Campbell, the other main contender, was too inexperienced. It was time for an Ontario leader with birth roots in Quebec and enough bilingual capacity to see the party through. Given the massive unpopularity of some of Mulroney's measures, the notion that the Tories might be returned to office seemed fanciful, but someone who knew the issues, was articulate in both languages, and had wide party experience might make a difference to a measured result. I gave the proposal serious thought, but in the end I declined it. There was a risk that Jean Charest, who was also considering running, might demur if I joined the contest, and I had no wish to stand in the way of someone whom I saw as an exciting candidate from Quebec.

But in 1997–98, when I did throw my hat in the ring, things were different. At that point, the Conservatives were in fifth place. Decimated by the Reform Party of Preston Manning and Lucien Bouchard's Bloc Québécois, the party was technically financially bankrupt. Because of the amazing opportunities it had afforded me to date, I decided this was precisely the time to give back.

My leadership campaign was spirited and policy-focused, including a proposal for a basic income policy. I centred my approach on defence and strategic priorities, a reduction in the GST, structural reforms to the federal government, and a fresh approach to poverty reduction.

I criss-crossed the country and met thousands of Progressive Conservatives during my campaign. But when Joe Clark entered the leadership race, the inclination of the membership was to give him a second chance. When the first-ballot results were announced, I held a respectable second place, and Clark was 2 percent shy of the required 50 percent plus 1. I suspect history will show that I was not as ruthless as required, that I was too policy-focused, and that, as my daughter commented, I was not sufficiently "vanilla" for what was left of the PC Party.

Though not problematic in terms of my larger career, my loss was a serious financial setback, because the funds raised had not covered all the campaign expenditures. Hundreds of thousands of dollars in debts needed to be paid. To my deep gratitude, many people from other parties also helped with a post-campaign fundraising dinner at the Harbour Castle in Toronto, and dear friends such as Harry Near, Bill Fox, and Michael Kirby soldiered on to get the debt down. What was left was a second mortgage on our home. The experience taught me plenty about my own imperfections and how focus on policy matters could be, on occasion, beside the point. Clark had won handily on the second ballot. I met with him at the Unity Dinner held at the Royal York afterward, offering to work alongside him, help politically, run for Parliament in Kingston, or, as is often most helpful, get out of the way. Not surprisingly, he chose the fourth option, which was his right as the duly elected leader. This ended my less-than-stellar career in elective Progressive Conservative politics.

▼

During my years at Queen's and in the private sector, I wrote, read, spoke, taught, and learned more about how a basic income program might best be put into effect. Serving as head of the Institute for Research on Public Policy (IRPP) in Montreal between 1999 and 2006, I worked with economists, social policy experts, governments, and think-tanks at home and abroad on a wide array of health planning, fiscal, monetary policy, defence, foreign policy, and trade issues. For me, the core question was always, "What can we do to reduce the pain and dislocation of poverty while expanding the economic mainstream?"

When Liberal prime minister Paul Martin began planning a first ministers' meeting on reinvesting in health care, the IRPP sought to serve its mandate of informing public debate by establishing a task force on health care. It was chaired by Monique Bégin, under whom the Canada Health Act had been introduced. Panellists included Duncan Sinclair, the dean of health science at Queen's; Michael Decter, former deputy minister of health for Ontario; Colleen Flood, a University of Toronto law professor who focused on health law; Henry Friesen, chair of Genome Canada's board; Carolyn Tuohy, a distinguished scholar and researcher in worldwide health policy; Claude Forget, a former deputy minister and minister of health in Quebec; and Maureen Quigley, a former senior policy officer in the Ontario Cabinet Office and respected consultant on health system governance issues. The task-force report was published in 2000 as a series of recommendations directed at provincial first ministers. My old colleague Graham Fox, now CEO of the IRPP, was the senior staffer holding the pen and directing much of the work.

The excellent conclusions of the task force regarding costs, comprehensiveness, accountability, and organization – including the oncoming demographic tsunami of senior citizens – convinced me that extending the time frame for people to live independently without the need for acute health care treatment was the best cost and logistics management strategy. Since poor people need more acute health care overall and suffer chronic diseases sooner than their better-off counterparts, reducing poverty was obviously the best health care policy choice that any rational government might pursue. Leaving millions of Canadians beneath the poverty line would diminish any and all other successes. Any discussion of health policy and reinvestment without addressing the social determinants of health is, simply, irrelevant.

CHAPTER 13

The Battle in the Senate

▼

Official dignity tends to increase

in inverse ratio to the importance of the country

in which the office is held.

ALDOUS HUXLEY

▲

WHEN I RECEIVED A CALL from Liberal prime minister Paul Martin in the summer of 2005, asking me to serve in the Senate, first I had to get over my surprise. The PM indicated that I could sit as a Conservative, a Progressive Conservative, a Liberal, or even an independent if that were my preference, and he gave me time to talk with my family before agreeing. Once I had chatted with Donna and Jacqueline, the thought of using my time as a senator to advance the two files I cared about most, income security at home and strategic security abroad, became too compelling to resist.

I told the prime minister that I would be honoured to serve, and that my preference, because I believed that Canadians should have at least two strong alternatives from which to choose at election time, was to sit with the Conservative Senate caucus. In 2005, the Red Chamber had a majority of Liberal senators. On the day of the announcement, I called Opposition leader Stephen Harper to ask if I might be welcome in his caucus. He was accepting, albeit clear about his belief that an unelected

Senate was, in the long run, not a healthy part of a parliamentary democracy. I had known Harper when he sat on the IRPP board, a position he held before I was chosen to be its president. His policy depth and principled sense of the public interest were never in doubt.

The day I was sworn in was a shiny mix of conflicting emotions. I was surrounded by all the wonderful people who care most about me and about whom I care most. After being introduced (I was one of several senators sworn in that day) and walking into the Senate to applause from both sides, I bowed to the Speaker and was invited to recite the oath of loyalty to Her Majesty. I put my hand on our old family Bible, the one I had used when I swore my oath of secrecy at Queen's Park and in the Privy Council Office when I became chief of staff to a prime minister. I hadn't expected to be fazed by the ceremony, but I was. As I sat down to sign the registry, at the table that held the mace representing the authority of the Crown, I couldn't help but think of my dad the cab driver and of my mom, who would have been so proud. I thought, too, of the bailiff coming to repossess our furniture and the sacrifice of my toy box so that another family might stay warm. What in the world was I doing here? There must be some mistake!

By the time I was led to my seat in the last row on the Opposition side of the House, to the Speaker's left, the lump in my throat was growing. I looked up at the Speaker's Gallery to see my family and closest friends in the world. I glanced up at the remarkable paintings portraying the suffering and sacrifices of so many in the First World War. As I put on my earpiece and wiped away a tear or two, I reminded myself that I was here because of the opportunities a great country had given to a poor, second-generation Canadian kid from very modest roots. There were millions of kids out there who deserved their own chance. I knew that was why I was here.

▼

Throughout my time in the Senate, from 2005 to 2014, various issues and debates drew me in. But there was one issue, of course, that remained central. Although I knew it was a long shot that I could change the minds or twist the arms of Ottawa policy-makers, I could certainly make noise in this new position. I had a moral duty to try!

In 1971, Senator David Croll, a former mayor of Windsor and provincial minister, had authored *Poverty in Canada: Report of the Special Senate Committee on Poverty*, an influential document and the first Senate report to call for a guaranteed annual income (GAI). An iconic report, it slammed the present welfare regimes for their inefficiency and stigmatization, showed that poverty had not improved at all, and explained why and how a GAI would be so much better.

One of my first tasks as a senator was to find out more about David Croll, who had died in 1991: who he was, why he had undertaken this particular study, and what his life had been like before he was appointed to the Senate. What I discovered about his personal and political history reminded me yet again that when you are doing genuine research, it is always useful to dig a little deeper. The importance of learning more about significant figures in history cannot be overstated, especially if you believe, as I do, that the better we understand history, the better our prospects for the future.

I learned from my research that David Croll was Canada's first Jewish senator, appointed in 1955 by Prime Minister Louis St. Laurent. Croll was popular, the only Liberal who won federal office in Toronto during the election of 1945, representing the tenderloin immigrant riding of Spadina. A two-time mayor of Windsor, he had won his seat in the Ontario legislature twice and had served with the Essex Scottish Regiment during the Second World War, rising from the rank of private to that of lieutenant-colonel. With a background like that, he was a natural for cabinet. However, St. Laurent was not about to appoint Canada's first Jewish federal cabinet minister.

As mayor of Windsor, Croll had taken the city into deficit to provide financial assistance for those suffering through the Depression. Appointed to the provincial Liberal cabinet of Mitch Hepburn, he resigned as labour minister when Hepburn dispatched the police and other hired auxiliaries to browbeat and harass strikers from General Motors. In resigning, Croll declared for all to hear, "I would rather walk with the workers than ride with General Motors." He would have been a welcome and cherished guest at my grandfather's Passover Seder table. His stance in championing a GAI in 1971 revealed him to be the sort of large servant of the greater good whose life one might seek to learn from but could never emulate. I vowed to study *Poverty in Canada,* which had been released three years after the Senate established the committee's terms of reference in November 1968 – six months after the election of the Trudeau government.

As I began my Senate work, I pursued a peripheral but not unrelated mission. It had to do with the late Robert Stanfield, an early promoter of the GAI. After he died in 2003, the Liberal government and airport authorities in Nova Scotia had unenthusiastically decided to rename the Terminal Building in Halifax. It would become the Robert Stanfield Terminal Building. Stanfield had been the seventeenth premier of Nova Scotia and a long-serving leader of the Opposition in the House of Commons. But the powers that be could not bring themselves to rechristen the entire airport in his honour? I, among many Canadians, was furious.

After I joined the Senate, it struck me that historical justice doesn't happen by accident. Sometimes, it needs a push. I met with the Halifax airport authorities. I lobbied both the Martin government and the incoming Harper administration after 2006. I spoke with the premier of Nova Scotia. In this effort, I was by no means alone. Senator James Cowan, a prominent Liberal from Nova Scotia and Liberal leader in the Senate, was unreservedly engaged. Peter MacKay, minister of defence and foreign affairs in the Harper government, was also on board. On February 9, 2007, Prime Minister Harper announced the renaming of Halifax International as the Robert L. Stanfield International Airport. Ideas that take courage to implement require people of principle and decency to launch them. If anyone should be commemorated, leaders of Stanfield's calibre should be.

During the rest of Paul Martin's term, I was a member of the Senate Committee on Agriculture and Forestry, chaired by Joyce Fairbairn of Alberta. I had known Fairbairn when she was Pierre Trudeau's legislative assistant in the 1968–75 period, while I was serving in the same role in Stanfield's office. She had been one of the first women to head a news bureau in the Parliamentary Press Gallery, and I knew her to be honourable and deeply focused on serving others. Coincidentally, Senator Fairbairn had also been the Canadian Press reporter whose *Winnipeg*

Free Press article covered the dilution of the GAI idea at the PC Party's Niagara conference in 1969.

The agriculture and forestry committee's vice-chair was Len Gustafson, a grain farmer and long-time former PC MP from Saskatchewan. Other members included the irrepressible George Baker, from Newfoundland and Labrador, who had been a Liberal cabinet minister, and Catherine Callbeck, also a Liberal. She was Canada's first elected female premier (of Prince Edward Island). They were joined by hockey star Frank Mahovlich and Terry Mercer, from Nova Scotia, a former YMCA CEO and national director of the Liberal Party. Also on the committee were Robert Peterson, an avuncular and totally decent farming and business leader from Saskatchewan, and my old friend Gerry St. Germain, former PC Party president and minister in the Mulroney cabinet. Joyce Fairbairn was a fair and completely non-partisan chair.

This committee provided my first chance in the Senate to try to advance the GAI cause. It was doing an inquiry into rural poverty, a reference from the Senate that I and others had encouraged. There was a genuine bi-partisan interest in exposing the reality of poverty in rural Canada, an area that is often underserved by social service and local health agencies, has problems with transportation, and lacks a steady economic base. Farming had become increasingly unsustainable unless someone also worked elsewhere, and fewer farms were being inherited or passed on within families.

Unlike in the city, where housing, crime, and service issues relating to poverty appear every night on the news, rural poverty is too often invisible to outsiders and ignored. Bucolic countryside drives can create the impression that everything is just fine. As our committee study revealed, this assumption is rarely justified. My own experience working on PEI issues with David MacDonald had underlined that reality.

One contribution that my office made was a study on access to health care in rural Ontario, conducted by Michelle Khan, a summer student and Loran Scholar at Queen's University. This study, which would be included as an appendix to the final committee report, illustrated only one among the many areas of difficulty for rural families with less than steady incomes.

The testimony that we committee members heard during our inquiry was about the increasing need for food banks, seniors isolated in their homes, problems with ambulance and fire services, and elevated poverty levels in rural communities. We also learned that some of the existing poverty and life needs indexes did not calibrate the realities of rural life.

We thus reviewed how many federal government assessments and popular indexes missed the full dimension of rural poverty. One index, for example, developed by an economist from Nipissing University, used a market-basket measure test to assess the cash needs of the rural poor. To determine what these might be, the test measures income against the cost of a basket of goods and services, such as food, rent, heat, clothing, and public transit. As this particular index set a lower annual minimum requirement than the standard "low-income cut-off measure" – less than half the median income – many conservative economists obviously preferred it. However, when one of the market-basket's leading proponents testified before us, we made a discovery. The measure had assumed that the public transit costs for rural residents were the same as those for city dwellers. The problem with this? In most parts of rural Canada, there is very little, if any, public transit. However old the family truck, sedan, or station wagon might be, it's the only option. When buses or cabs are simply not available, there is no other choice, and even the basic cost of running a vehicle and paying for insurance dwarfs the price of subway tokens or bus fare. Under gentle questioning, the economist admitted that the calculation might be off on that one measure.

After many weeks, the committee report was prepared and sent to the Senate for debate. Disappointingly, I had not been able to convince my colleagues that a firm recommendation for a GAI made sense. Senators tend to be conservative, and some committee members could not be persuaded to relinquish the notion that poverty is the result of laziness. A recommendation that a Green Paper on a GAI be prepared did make the cut, along with a wide range of recommendations on rural infrastructure, spreading public works more evenly across regionalized government departments, and improving Internet access. I viewed my colleagues on the committee, all of whom had far more experience than I did in Senate work, as thoroughly decent and fair-minded. But on fundamental welfare reform and poverty reduction, they were still back in the 1960s. In the end, our report endorsed a pilot project for a GAI as one of various soft options.

The report, entitled *Beyond Freefall: Halting Rural Poverty*, was released in June 2008. It was progress but not very much. It did allow members of the committee, such as Gerry St. Germain and Terry Mercer, to reflect publicly on our substantive findings, both across Canada and in Senate debates. One committee member who cared deeply about the issue of rural poverty was Catherine Callbeck, who brought to her work a granular and humane sense of what low-income Prince Edward Islanders faced. She was deeply respected at home and bi-partisan in her disposition on issues, especially in defence of seniors facing economic challenges. Her anxieties about a GAI were related to the risk that it could be seen as paying people to do nothing. I would hear this concern from many sources over the years. Occasionally, it was expressed by the mean-spirited or the ideologically narrow, but on the whole it was grounded in the Protestant work ethic, which is so much a part of the Canadian social and economic fabric – not in itself a bad thing, but with respect to the low-income community, a misplaced fear.

In Ontario, for example, 12 to 15 percent of residents were living beneath the poverty line, but a full 70 percent of them had jobs. Many had more than one. Most worked for minimum wage, an income far too small for them to escape poverty. For those on welfare/income security/ Ontario Works, the monthly amount was both well beneath the poverty line and encumbered with rules that deeply discouraged work. For any income earned over a very small limit, their benefits would be cut back dollar-for-dollar. Try as I would, I failed to convince most of my Senate colleagues that an automatic basic income top-up, like the guaranteed annual income supplement the Davis government had brought in for seniors during the mid-1970s, would do more to encourage work and reduce poverty than present provincial programs. I viewed the report's tepid final recommendation, not as their mistake, but as my failure. I would have to find more compelling and effective ways to advance the cause.

▼

Art Eggleton, a former mayor of Toronto and former minister of defence under Jean Chrétien, played a leadership role in helping to bring the Senate to a more coherent conclusion. He chaired the Subcommittee on Cities, with a focus on urban poverty, which was a part of his Standing

Committee on Social Affairs, Science and Technology. I was a member of that committee, as well as the Senate Committee on Foreign Affairs and International Trade. The Subcommittee on Cities was struck in February 2009, and I was asked to be its vice-chair.

By then, I had made a close reading of *Poverty in Canada,* the 1971 Croll Report. Its arrival in the aftermath of the War Measures Act of late fall 1970 had dampened its impact, but the first paragraph of its introduction said it all: "The time has come to stop blaming the mirror for not being a window, for presenting us with things we would rather not see. The time has come for a little common honesty. The poor, after all, are not, as some still pretend, poor of their own accord. The poor have no uncommon moral flaw that sets them apart, let alone condemns them. They are casualties of the way we manage our economy and our society – and that fact is increasingly obvious to the poor themselves."

After three years of deliberation, many hearings, and dozens of written submissions on everything from defining the poverty line, education, health care, community support, and legal aid, Croll's Senate committee issued thirty-eight recommendations, covering economic policy and applied social research in the stated areas and more. But its most salient recommendation was for a GAI to address the central issue of poverty – that the poor did not have enough funds to meet their basic food, housing, clothing, transportation, and heating requirements with any sense of self-respect or assurance.

The Croll Report was precise and clear in its call "that the Government of Canada implement a Guaranteed Annual Income (G.A.I.) program using the Negative Income Tax (N.I.T.) method, on a uniform, national basis." The report also suggested that the GAI be set at 70 percent of the poverty line. Most welfare programs paid less than 40 or 50 percent.

As chair of the Senate Subcommittee on Cities, Art Eggleton was generous and bi-partisan. When he was mayor of Toronto, he had racked up the best record on social housing investment of any mayor in the city's history. Though not perfect as defence minister (who could be?), he had invested heavily in housing, facilities, and salaries for our women and men in uniform. He also found a way to keep the under-the-sea part of our navy alive; had he not procured second-hand submarines from the United Kingdom, that would have been the end of Canada's submarine history.

The work of our Subcommittee on Cities was unique in many ways. We visited communities and listened intently to those with "lived poverty" experience across Canada, including among First Nations. My work with that group was one of the most interesting and inspiring assignments I could have.

Rosemarie Brisson, who worked with me as a senior policy advisor, researcher, and writer, was instrumental in two key parts of this committee's work. Rose was from Cornwall, Ontario, but she had lived in Kingston as a Queen's student and had moved back to Kingston with her family in 1988. She was active in the theatre community there and had worked with Peter Milliken, the local Liberal MP and longest-serving Speaker of the House. In her native Cornwall, Rose had been a loyal volunteer for Ed Lumley, senior minister in various Liberal governments. As a young person in Cornwall, she had met Pierre Trudeau, and to this day she remains more Liberal than Conservative most of the time.

I had first met Rose when her friend Helen Cooper, the former mayor of Kingston, sought and won the PC federal nomination before the 1997 general election. Rose helped every inch of the way with Cooper's uphill but spirited and well-run campaign. Also during that year, under Jean Charest's inspired leadership, my own party fought its way back from the precipice of oblivion, moving from two seats under Kim Campbell in 1993 to regaining formal party status with twenty seats. I was one of many volunteers in Kingston whom Rose organized and motivated. She was engaging, focused, and no-nonsense. Helen Cooper did well, though not quite well enough to get her over the top in what had then become a public-sector union town. In the 1988 election, the amazing Flora MacDonald, Canada's first female foreign minister, was defeated by Milliken in a seat she had held since 1972. A decade later, during my 1998 run for the Tory leadership, Helen Cooper chaired my local leadership campaign, and Rose ran it. Outside of one Quebec riding, where my votes were inexplicably higher, Kingston was my best Canadian riding – over 65 percent – despite heavy establishment Joe Clark forces.

When I was appointed to the Senate, I knew I needed someone with Rose Brisson's intensity, competence, and writing skills. She had a secure public-sector job with the provincial government at the time and a deeply rooted Kingston life, where she led the Domino Theatre association and was active in many fields. The sacrifice of moving to Ottawa for a few days a week for the new junior senator from Ontario (Kingston-Frontenac-Leeds) must have been onerous. But whatever I might have achieved in the Senate, substantive or otherwise, Rose's decision to take on the job was the most seminal constructive force in making it possible.

While researching in support of the Subcommittee on Cities, Rose came across a small Manitoba newspaper article that mentioned Evelyn Forget and described Forget's acquisition of 1,800 boxes of forgotten data from a thirty-five-year-old government experiment. Forget was a health economics professor at the University of Manitoba Health Science Centre, and the newspaper story said she was researching a 1970s GAI pilot project known as Mincome. Rose brought the article to the subcommittee's attention and insisted that Forget be invited to one of the Saturday morning expert roundtables Senator Eggleton and I convened from time to time.

When Dr. Forget duly gave her presentation, we learned that in the mid-1970s, the Ed Schreyer government in Manitoba and the Trudeau government in Ottawa had collaborated on a basic income top-up program in Dauphin, Manitoba, and parts of Winnipeg. In typical Canadian fashion, the program operated for a few years and then came to an end, in part because of a new austerity agreement among the G8 countries and the defeat of Pierre Trudeau by Joe Clark in 1979. Premier Schreyer had been defeated by Sterling Lyon and the Progressive Conservatives in 1977, as well.

That the two Conservative Parties had moved away from a program initiated by the Liberals and New Democrats was not surprising. But the fact that no assessment or cost-benefit analysis of effect had been done for Mincome was simply scandalous. Evelyn Forget had taken on the task of righting this wrong, working with a few graduate students. Using empirical methodology, she meticulously went through thousands of anonymized records, Manitoba health insurance files, and other indicators of community and workplace impact to produce a careful set of studies on the real effect of the Mincome test. Her conclusions, that an automatic top-up for those beneath the poverty line had not only not discouraged work but had reduced health costs and other negatives produced by poverty, greatly influenced how members of our subcommittee saw the issues.

Rose Brisson's down-to-earth approachability also brought the committee's work into contact with some hard truths. One week, I was in Halifax, where I was slated to meet up with subcommittee members who had been holding hearings in Newfoundland. Before our formal hearings began in Halifax, we were scheduled to hold an informal discussion in a Catholic facility for young single mothers and their children. When fog kept the committee members stranded in Newfoundland, Rose and I went to the facility on our own. It provided small but comfortable apartments, daycare, and other support services, and it seemed both humane and considerate. The reality of being a single parent, trying to look after the child, find work, and survive on an inadequate welfare stipend, was described to us in some detail. (In truth, there are too few facilities like this one, but that is an entirely different story.)

After a roundtable discussion, Rose took a smoke break with some of the young mothers. That was where she heard about a practice of local welfare officials at the time. It seems they were desperate to discover who had fathered the children of these women. Why? To make them pay support – not to add to the income of mother and child, but to reduce how much support the Province paid the mother. You can't make this stuff up! Rose learned that the Province pressured the young mothers to disclose the identity of the father. Many had made a conscious decision to move on from the men in question, often for good and substantial reasons. But until 2010, that was the practice. Nova Scotia wanted names, and the government was willing to pay for DNA tests to determine paternity. We could not have collected this kind of on-the-ground information without Rose's engagement and commitment on the file.

Our subcommittee report, *In from the Margins: A Call to Action on Poverty, Housing and Homelessness,* was released on December 2, 2009. Its list of final recommendations called for the establishment of a pilot GAI project, along with wholesale reform. The report went on to become a touchstone for anti-poverty groups, various church organizations, and the Conference Board of Canada, which had been making the case for a GAI for some time. It also cemented my deep respect for the remarkable work that Evelyn Forget had done, and continued to do, in charting poverty's impact on difficult health outcomes.

The Senate subcommittee members had worked seamlessly to produce the final draft of the report. Sadly, though comprehensive on everything from First Nations to housing, training, and seniors' income supplements, the report was weak-kneed on the issue of a GAI. There were strange points of disagreement among committee members. Willy Keon, a distinguished heart surgeon and long-time senator from Ottawa (appointed by Mulroney to help ensure the passage of the GST through the Senate), argued against the relationship between poverty and ill health. To prove his claim, he cited Cuba's comprehensive health care system, of all things. I am still puzzled by the logic in that argument. Senator Eggleton, who generally was a leader and proponent of many changes to afford low-income Canadians a shot at a better life, could not bring himself to embrace a GAI as a core, undiluted recommendation at that time. This was despite the fact that at its national policy conferences, the Liberal Party had proposed a guaranteed annual income several times. Our report's fifth recommendation, that Ottawa should "further examine a basic annual income based on a negative income tax," struck me as feeble and a little less than had been recommended by Senator Croll's committee in 1971. Many of the recommendations in *In from the Margins* were carefully crafted to deal with contradictions and snafus in federal programming that hurt the poor and ended up being counterproductive in operation, and the subcommittee deserved immense credit for those. Its failure to engage fully on the GAI choice, however, weakened the report's finding that little progress had been made on the poverty issue during the decades since the Croll Report.

I had lost the battle on the urban poverty side, just as I had lost the battle on rural poverty. I was not losing the argument against people who didn't care about the poor; all my colleagues on both committees genuinely did care. I was losing the battle with decent and accomplished senators who were afflicted with what I call "programitis." When agencies and government departments appear before any Senate committee, they naturally speak about how their programs are supposed to be working. Senators naturally probe to determine what is working and what isn't. They ask questions about whether the agencies actually are progressing toward their goals and about how performance could be improved or value for taxpayers' money increased. This happens in the House of

Commons as well as the Senate, as it does before provincial legislative committees across Canada.

The core problem with this approach is that it assumes there are programmatic responses to poverty that can defeat it: a better designed housing subsidy, well-supplied food banks, or enhanced training programs. Yet the central issue for the poor is lack of money. In most provinces, welfare systems still pay less than 50 percent of the poverty line. Concentrating on program-design issues misses this central reality. But I had failed to convince my colleagues, and the frustration was very painful. I would continue to engage on the poverty file in other ways. I would also conclude that we in the Senate took ourselves a touch too seriously. Of course, taking your work seriously is as important as respecting your colleagues, even those with whom you disagree. But being afraid to embrace the risk of policy change because you sit in the comfortable pew of inertia, because someone might disagree, or because you might face criticism is a symptom of excessive self-reverence.

▼

In 2009, I was nominated by the Department of Foreign Affairs and International Trade to sit as the Canadian representative on the Commonwealth Eminent Persons Group (EPG). Appointments to the group were formally made and announced by Kamalesh Sharma, secretary-general of the Commonwealth. Other countries represented at the EPG table were Malaysia, Ghana, Jamaica, Pakistan, the United Kingdom, Uganda, Australia, Kiribati, and Antigua and Barbuda. Our remit was reform and modernization of the Commonwealth and its Secretariat, headquartered in Marlborough House in London, to better address the genuine needs of the fifty-three countries and 2.3 billion human beings within its reach.

The Commonwealth grouping comprises some of the wealthiest countries in the world (the United Kingdom, Canada, Australia, New Zealand, Singapore) and some of the poorest (Mozambique, Sierra Leone, Bangladesh, Pakistan, and Tanzania). What struck me immediately was its serious lack of engagement in lifting its millions of poor people out of poverty. The Commonwealth does not have binding treaties or a narrow mission such as trade or defence, but it does have a plethora of global organizations: law societies, nursing educational associations, bar associations, and universities among others. In a world where the gap between the wealthiest and the poorest is growing, my view was that the Commonwealth should be an informed and instrumental advocate for North-South cooperation and genuine action on alleviating poverty. Small island states, for example, which make up half of the Commonwealth's fifty-three members, face serious issues of development, poverty, and rising sea levels. In some countries, including the Maldives, Sri Lanka, and Bangladesh, these problems have created a destabilizing effect. Parts of Africa, Asia, and the Caribbean face similar challenges.

The Commonwealth country with the largest population is also the largest democracy on the planet, India. Its success in lifting millions of people out of abject poverty into a growing middle class is impressive. In Asia, India is in competition with the Chinese model, which, though also impressive in terms of economic progress, is utterly devoid of room for dissent, a free press, competitive political parties, or ethnic diversity. For me, that underlined even more acutely the role the Commonwealth should play in the global forums where fifty-three countries could be effective if seeking to promote shared priorities.

I also suffered from the nostalgic notion that, just as Prime Ministers Diefenbaker, Trudeau, and Mulroney had agreed on the need to defeat apartheid in South Africa, the present generation of Commonwealth leaders would be determined to combat the forces that were limiting human rights, the rule of law, and the other key instruments that were essential to hope and economic and social progress. In Africa, some countries were actually reinstating old colonial anti-sodomy laws, which put their gay populations at serious risk of life and limb. In countries where presidents served in perpetuity, economic levers never opened to let genuine opportunity prevail. Across the Commonwealth, half of the population was under thirty-five years of age, and yet more than half of those young people were unemployed. When freedom from want is addressed for those who have been disenfranchised, they are less likely to choose violence, terrorism, gang, or other criminal activities.

The Eminent Persons Group worked together over many months of discussion and research, meeting in London and Kuala Lumpur. We produced a robust reform agenda that focused on the needs of small island nations, countries lacking economic stability, and those with poor human rights records. We proposed an enhanced role for the Commonwealth in terms of both youth economic development and the creation of a commissioner for human rights, democracy, and the rule of law. Our collective thinking was that the only sanction the Commonwealth could impose was the withdrawal or suspension of membership. Nelson Mandela had brought the Republic of South Africa back into the Commonwealth when democracy was reinstated there with majority rule. Nigeria had been suspended when a military junta took over but had sought and received readmission as soon as democracy was restored. The same had happened with Pakistan. It was clear that member nations saw their linkage with the Commonwealth as constructive and of diplomatic and economic value. They also appreciated their regular meetings with the head of the Commonwealth, Her Majesty, who had always made it one of her primary concerns.

The completed EPG report, *A Commonwealth of the People: Time for Urgent Reform,* was endorsed at the Commonwealth Heads of Government Meeting (CHOGM) in Perth, Australia, in 2011, except for its proposal on a commissioner for human rights, democracy, and the rule of law. The dynamic here was fascinating, because it turned out that Secretary-General Kamalesh Sharma had been playing both sides. While vocally supportive of our work, he had also been quietly assuring horrific authoritarians in Uganda, Sri Lanka, and elsewhere that the report's human rights proposition would not pass. Before the Perth CHOGM, I and other EPG members had met with Commonwealth foreign ministers on the margins of the annual United Nations General Assembly in New York. We had a vigorous discussion about how many of our report's recommendations might work, but there was no opposition to the human rights proposal, as long as the Commonwealth Ministerial Action Group and the secretary-general were mandated to make all final decisions relating to suspension or sanction. This had always been the plan.

I was proud of the Government of Canada for standing firm on this file. Prime Minister Harper and Foreign Minister John Baird were resolute and determined. In fact, it was Harper who, in posing a "Where are you actually?" question to Secretary-General Sharma in Perth, exposed his hypocrisy and double game. Our report was presented by the distinguished and prudent Tun Abdullah Ahmad Badawi, former prime minister of

Malaysia, who chaired the EPG. When Harper's question revealed the duplicity of Sharma, Badawi, with great dignity, informed Sharma that he had let down the volunteers who had put in so much time on the report and, in the process, the millions of residents in Commonwealth countries.

There was also another game in play. Despite the ongoing violence against Tamil civilians and journalists, and the suppression of economic and political rights in the Tamil north of the country, Sri Lanka was chosen as the location for the next CHOGM. Various countries, including Canada, opposed this choice. Several years had elapsed since the Sri Lankan civil war had ended, and yet there had been no reconciliation, no findings regarding the atrocities that had been committed on both sides. A pervasive culture of impunity, sustained by the Sinhalese majority government in Colombo, allowed the oppression of the Tamil north.

In anticipation of the next CHOGM, and in light of Canada's opposition to the location, Foreign Minister John Baird asked me to become Canada's special envoy to the Commonwealth on reform and human rights. My work on his behalf simply confirmed the relationship between poverty and violence. I travelled to South Africa, Malaysia, Singapore, Bangladesh, Sri Lanka, Kenya, India, Maldives, Trinidad, and the United Kingdom, making representations to governments, parliamentary committees, and the media in support of the need for the Commonwealth, as outlined by the EPG report, to step up to this challenge.

I observed first-hand the results of the situation in Jaffna, a city in northern Sri Lanka, where President Mahinda Rajapaksa's regime was determined to keep the Tamil population poor and without hope. But I also witnessed the outstanding work of institutions such as the Aga Khan's schools in the poorest areas of Tanzania, the goal being the alleviation of poverty through excellent education opportunities.

My visit to Sri Lanka, at the invitation of its foreign minister, G.L. Peiris, was revealing in many ways. I was accompanied by Rosemarie Brisson and Assistant Deputy Minister (South Asia) Peter Bates, and we were aided immensely by Canada's courageous high commissioner to Sri Lanka, Shelley Whiting.

Whiting's previous posting had been Bosnia, so she was familiar with challenging assignments. In Colombo, she had been given the cold shoulder by the Sri Lankan government, which was headed by the Rajapaksa family, because of Canada's position of principle. The family's Sinhalese party had won a large majority – more than two-thirds of the Sri Lankan Parliament – but the fact that the prime minister, defence minister, economic development minister, and Speaker of Parliament were brothers struck me as a whole new definition of "family compact." The end of the civil war, with its ruthless Tamil Tiger separatist armies, was a matter of justifiable relief for the entire population. The Tamil Tigers had perfected the suicide bomber tactic, and they rained down havoc on civilian Sri Lankan communities.

The end of the war understandably afforded the Rajapaksa administration great credit. Not so the way in which the conflict had ended. For example, Tamil civilians and combatants had been encouraged to surrender and proceed to a no-fire safe zone that was then bombarded by Sri Lankan army artillery, killing thousands in violation of every Geneva Convention provision possible. The absence of any accounting for such measures meant that no progress toward truth and reconciliation had taken place. Forces associated with the Colombo government had engaged in the "white vanning" of journalists, dissidents, and others – grabbing individuals off the street and throwing them into a white van, after which they were never seen again. That, and the lack of effort to bring war criminals on either side to justice, had left a lot of unanswered questions and pots that threatened to boil over. No Tamils had been allowed to return to their farming or ancestral homes. The Sri Lankan military's control of the Tamil north was total.

When Rose Brisson, Shelley Whiting, Peter Bates, and I flew north from Colombo, we had to land at a military base near Jaffna because no civilian planes were allowed to land elsewhere. Our purpose was to meet with the leadership of the Sri Lanka Armed Forces, get a detailed briefing on security issues and economic development, and then proceed to meet with Tamil and Sri Lankan communities and government officials in the region. The Sri Lankan foreign minister had encouraged us to go anywhere and meet with anyone we chose. Our itinerary included the military, the Roman Catholic clergy, a Tamil-owned newspaper, local civil libertarians, a Tamil reconciliation committee, and members of the Sri Lankan Bar Association.

When we landed, we were briefed on three dimensions. First, as in Colombo, we were being monitored by the Sri Lankan authorities. At a luncheon in the official Canadian residence in Colombo, where we hosted a broad multicultural group of eminent Sri Lankans, plainclothes police had jotted down the licence numbers of our guests. Second, before our visit, Canadian government funds had been invested in two projects: de-mining areas heavily mined by both sides during the civil war so that the land could again be habitable or arable; and the translation into Tamil of the work of a parliamentary commission that had made some construct-ive recommendations after the war. We were informed that nothing had come of the recommendations, and as so often when land in the north was de-mined, signs had gone up indicating that it had been expropri-ated by the Sri Lanka Armed Forces for new bases and military barracks. And third, the military was seeking to control any commercially viable facility in the north to generate revenue for itself and to keep the Tamil population from returning.

Following the briefing, we were told that our military escort would take us, not to the region's military HQ, but to a new military-owned hotel in an adjacent area. We refused to change our plans, with the security/logistics officer from our High Commission indicating that we would willingly wait all day in our cars on the tarmac if necessary. In the end, the Sri Lankans gave in. A photograph of the Canadian high commissioner, a visiting Canadian special envoy, and other officials at a military-owned hotel for an official meeting in the Tamil region would have conferred legitimacy on the Rajapaksa regime's strategy of occupy-ing Tamil territory in perpetuity.

We visited with an elected MP from the Tamil National Alliance who owned a newspaper and had our discussions under bullet holes on the inside walls. Later that week, the paper would be invaded by government-related toughs, who shot up computers and beat employees. Intimidation was an ongoing theme.

Accompanied by UN high commissioner for refugees staff members, we visited the killing fields of Kilinochchi, where so many Tamils had died. We met with mothers, daughters, sisters, and wives of the executed, in spotless dirt-floor houses where they were kept waiting with the prom-ise of return to their own land. One household of two sisters told us they had been offered better housing if they signed away their rights to their homes in the north, something they were honour-bound not to do. Even though the women had to walk for a day to get food and half a day to get water, we noticed a small well-tended garden plot with local seasonal flowers. Rose asked one of the women why she would keep a flower garden when water was so precious and required such labour to fetch. Our translator posed the question, and the woman smiled. "Because this is our home," we were told. The Rajapaksa regime's purpose was to keep the Tamil population as poor as possible for as long as possible while moving in Sinhalese Buddhists to outnumber the Tamils in their own historic region of the country. Poverty was being used to destroy spirit and will.

▼

In my involvement with the Senate's anti-poverty committee and my work as special envoy to the Commonwealth, I saw time and time again how closely freedom from fear and freedom from want are connected. From the northern part of Sri Lanka to Malaysia, from Tanzania to Vancouver's Downtown Eastside, if basic income needs are not addressed, all the pathologies of poverty – ill health, poor education outcomes, substance abuse, and enhanced conditions for criminal activity – will ensue. Poverty is a universal abuser. First Nations, recent immigrants, developing democracies, and people of all races and colours are fodder for the mill of injustice and pain. And the heightened opportunities for terrorists, criminal gangs, and dictators to capitalize on the realities and fears of poverty should never be underestimated.

My policy work as a senator on poverty and global security was a treasured privilege. Deepening my understanding of how issues of want connect with threats to local and global security was just one benefit of being allowed to work on domestic poverty, international affairs, and terrorism prevention at the same time.

I will admit to shamelessly using my Senate position as a podium to champion a GAI, in an attempt to sway those who had the real clout in shaping policy. During my nine years in the Senate, I gave more than seventy-five speeches on the subject, did countless media interviews, wrote op-eds, attended small gatherings in church basements, and delivered keynote addresses at international conferences. Some attendees at those events were, like me, lifelong advocates of a GAI. Others had never heard of the concept. Though it was always heartening to speak with those who thought as I did, it was far more rewarding to change a mind or two about achieving a real solution to poverty at home and abroad.

I enjoyed my time in the Senate – most days. But by late 2013, it was mired in excessive partisan bickering and the wilful destruction of reputations by its Tory majority, which had become almost psychotic in its slavish loyalty to its helicopter parents in the Prime Minister's Office, who were meddling incompetently and somewhat maliciously in Senate affairs. And when the presumption of innocence and due process were suspended with regard to three senators, I found myself largely isolated in standing against it. Earlier that year, I had joined the opposition to a horrific private member's bill from the House that would essentially reduce the right to free collective bargaining for unions, by imposing financial disclosure rules under the Tax Act. Amendments to the act would force unions to publically disclose their financial information, a stipulation that would not apply to employers or corporations. The Tory rump in the House, made up largely of the anti-abortion cabal who had been frustrated by Harper's steadfast refusal to revive the matter, was encouraged from high up to pursue this base-delighting, anti-union effort. In the end, the bill was stopped by my colleagues on all sides of the House, great committee work, and a genuine strong and effective presence in debates and hearings by public and private union leadership. But I was at odds with most of my Tory colleagues in the House and the Senate.

In October 2013, the Conservative government's Senate House leader, Claude Carignan, proposed a motion to suspend three senators for gross negligence. On November 5, I was the only Conservative senator to vote against this measure. Senators Pamela Wallin, Mike Duffy, and Patrick Brazeau faced sloppy, unfair, and contrived allegations by a Tory partisan-majority committee, who denied their counsels the right to appear or ask questions. It was a monstrous violation of their recourse rights. The private member's bill and the treatment of the three senators made me wonder if the party's long-time association with fairness, due process, presumption of innocence, and fair rights for all sides of the economic framework was no longer mainstream in the 2013 federal Conservative Party. I knew where Bill Davis, Brian Mulroney, John Diefenbaker, Jean Charest, and Claude Wagner would have stood on these sorts of issues, but for whatever reason, the present leadership of the federal Tory party was no longer there. It was time, perhaps, for me to move on.

The situation reeked of the petty jealousies that can infect any small chamber of self-reverential people, especially since the Prime Minister's Office of the day had neither the perspective nor the constitutional expertise that would allow the Senate to properly address the alleged improprieties. When I sat down after that vote, I wondered if I were the only Conservative in the Senate who believed in presumption of innocence and due process. What was I doing there? Was the Senate still the place for me? As it turned out, a new path would soon open up ahead.

CHAPTER 14

Testing a Better Way

▼

Durability is one of the chief elements
of strength. Nothing is either loved or feared
but that which is likely to endure.

ALEX DE TOCQUEVILLE

▲

IN 2014, JOHN FRASER announced his impending departure as the fourth
master of Toronto's Massey College. He had held the job for a remarkable
two decades and, by many accounts, had done well. When University
Affairs advertised for a replacement, various people at the college encouraged me to respond.

Massey is a unique graduate residential college at, but independent
from, the University of Toronto. Its commitment to encouraging graduate
students in the sciences, humanities, arts, and professional and business
programs to learn from exposure to each other's disciplines had genuine
appeal for me. I knew that Massey had a modest program focused on
cultural, artistic, and intellectual activities that served to broaden the
interests of its junior fellows. Senior fellows and a non-academic cohort
of Quadrangle Society members added to the mix. As I considered the
possibility of applying, I reflected on whether I might contribute any
value to this important mission.

From the conversations I had, my sense was of an institution with compelling values, a strong association with the world of books and music, and many junior and senior fellows of achievement and genuine distinction. The college pursued its activities with a touch of whimsy and slightly over-the-top Oxbridge ceremony. I learned it was non-denominational but nominally Anglican, celebrating Christmas, Passover, and Hanukkah. It had an active chapel community, a commitment to chorale and instrumental music, and a rich calendar of events centred on public policy, seasonal celebrations, and bi-monthly high table dinners. Although aspects of the place were a little clubby and Rosedale liberal for my working-class tastes, the general mix seemed congenial. Home to the Southam journalism fellowships, the college was a partner in the annual CBC Radio Massey Lectures, which are broadcast on *Ideas* and published by House of Anansi Press. The thought of encouraging young people to reach out to the broader world, make linkages, and engage reminded me of the many happy years I spent teaching at the Policy Studies Graduate School and the Smith Business School at Queen's and, for a short while, at the University of Toronto Law School. When I applied for the position of master, I was genuinely surprised to survive to the short list of candidates and pleased to be invited to appear before the search committee.

When I left the Senate to become head of Massey College in 2014, I naturally assumed that any chance to continue my advocacy for a basic income would be limited to non-existent. I did resolve to use my influence to ensure as best I could that applicants to the college would be accepted on merit, without regard to what they could afford – a micro but important focus.

My first-year cycle as principal of the college (a title still styled then as "master") caught me up in many new tasks, one of which was identifying distinguished scholars on their sabbatical year who might be invited to live at Massey, continue their research, and interact with the college community, especially the junior fellows. For graduate students who aspire to lives as professors and scholars, the reduction of academic appointment opportunities means connections to government, the private sector, and the non-profit sector are all vital for career building.

In July 2014, I was invited to speak on a panel at a Literary Review of Canada event in Winnipeg, along with former premier and governor general Ed Schreyer and economist Evelyn Forget. The subject was Mincome, the 1975–78 GAI experiment in Manitoba: what had been learned from the pilot project and what could be applied to the future.

Prior to the session, Evelyn and I met for breakfast at the Fort Garry hotel. We reminisced a bit about the work of the Senate Subcommittee on Cities and reflected on where the debate about poverty reduction choices was headed in both Canada and elsewhere.

Then Evelyn said the magic words: "Hugh, I'm hoping to do more work on this file when my sabbatical starts in September."

"Where are you doing that sabbatical?" I asked.

"Not sure yet."

"How about Massey College?" I suggested.

After the necessary approvals, including the generosity of Tom Kierans and Mary Janigan, key supporters of the college, Evelyn Forget was designated the Kierans-Janigan visiting scholar for 2015–16. She was a stellar, warm, and engaged addition to the college community.

Within ten days of her arrival, I received a call from James Janeiro, a senior advisor on social policy in Premier Kathleen Wynne's office, asking if Evelyn and I might join the premier for coffee. The government was interested in improving its response to the challenges of poverty in Ontario and wanted to benefit from Evelyn's insights and experience. During the meeting, Evelyn explained how Mincome had worked, what the takeaways were for design and impact, and where poverty reduction needed to head.

The term "poverty reduction" is important here. Most welfare programs in Canada are not about poverty reduction. With support levels at about 40 percent of the poverty line, and precise disincentives to work ensconced in most program rules, welfare keeps people in poverty, offering very little real assistance. For one of my speeches, Rose Brisson had come up with the apt construct that the welfare safety net was like a spider's web – "strong enough to entangle, too weak to lift."

A basic income top-up works by reducing the number of poor people as a percentage of the total population. Since poverty is a sadly accurate and almost perfect predictor of poor health, low educational achievement for families, increased substance abuse, early need for hospital care, and unconstructive engagement with the law and the judicial system, it costs

Canada billions of dollars every year, independent of the actual outlays for welfare-based income security band-aids. Premier Wynne and her advisors seemed genuinely interested in using what Evelyn Forget had done to encourage new thinking on the file.

The provincial budget of spring 2016 saw the Ontario minister of finance, Charles Sousa, commit to a basic income pilot project for the coming year. I was delighted to hear the news, as were Evelyn and the many groups and organizations that supported the concept, including the Canadian Basic Income Network and Canada without Poverty.

I did not imagine that the minister's announcement had anything to do with me. Someone in government, however, decided that it should be my job to prepare the rationale and design for the pilot project and to set out its core principles and premises. I had not anticipated this assignment, but I had spent my whole adult life campaigning on this file, in both partisan and non-partisan terms. The premier of Canada's largest province, with the country's biggest, most diverse economy and population, had asked for my help. My only possible answer was yes.

The Wynne government was neither perfect nor Tory. Few governments of any persuasion are perfect, though, and few Conservative governments in Canada are "Tory" anymore. Today, when I use the word, I refer to a Disraeli-like belief in "one nation" politics – a politics that sees as unacceptable the vast difference between those living happy, well-funded lives of travel and luxury and a sub-culture in which people are denied enough to eat, indoor plumbing, time for family, or any enjoyment at all. A Tory respects tradition and the rule of law but sees the reduction of the gap between rich and poor as essential to his or her mission. The Disraeli administration made progress around child labour laws, breaks during the working day, a full weekend off, and other amenities for workers that reduced the pain and hopelessness of poverty. This is what I refer to when I use the word "Tory."

My suggested role in relation to the Ontario pilot would be non-partisan, and my report would be public domain. I gratefully received permission from Alan Broadbent, my board chair at Massey College, and Ian Webb, the audit committee chair with whom I had negotiated my employment contract, to take on the work during my holiday time between terms. Aside from travel expenses, used largely to meet with officials in Ottawa and with anti-poverty advocates and social service agencies across the province, I neither sought nor received compensation from Queen's Park. My political experience had taught me that, in today's media world, any answer other than "zero" to the question "How much is this former senator being paid to help the poor?" would be seriously problematic and an unhealthy diversion from the task at hand.

My work began in May 2016, with the inspired assistance of Maripier Isabelle, a junior fellow at Massey. Maripier had been recommended by Rose Brisson, who worked at Massey for two years in Alumni and Quad-rangler Relations and became a go-to person for many junior fellows seeking clear-cut and confidential life advice. As a brilliant doctoral can-didate in health economics, Maripier combined her passion for social justice and public policy with the acute methodological discipline and knowledge of her métier. Her thesis advisor was Mark Stabile, also an economist, the first head of the School of Public Policy and Governance at the University of Toronto and someone who had done extensive work on income distribution, health impacts, and linkages. Maripier had been an active youth leader in the Quebec Liberal Party (I forgave her for that) and was an inspirational leader in the college life at Massey.

As is the case with any assignment, getting a handle on my actual role was the first order of the day. The advocates for the pilot project were senior ministers of the Ontario government. These included Helena Jaczek, the minister of community and social services, who had been a distinguished epidemiologist before entering politics; Deputy Premier Deb Matthews, a former health minister, who had been assigned a key anti-child-poverty role in the early days of the government; and Minister of Health Eric Hoskins, a strong promoter of upstream investment to reduce the health impacts of poverty. All were very supportive, as were the premier, her senior staff, and other public servants.

My job, I determined, was to shape a plan, a framework, and a series of governing premises and principles that would map out why a pilot was necessary, exactly what it should test and not test, where and how it should take place, how it might best be administered, and what kind of evidence the government, the legislature, and the public had the right to expect before deciding whether to replace welfare with something demonstrably better.

Vital here was understanding precisely what "better" meant. The government had helped define that by including a statement in its spring 2016 budget. It was trying to determine if there were a way to abate poverty that was less stigmatizing, more encouraging of work, and more likely to produce better health and education outcomes for low-income Ontarians than Ontario Works (welfare) and the Ontario Disability Support Program (ODSP).

What we knew of the existing system was public record. It cost the Province about $9 billion annually. It was very rules-based, involving heavy caseloads for the public servants who administered Ontario Works and the ODSP. Program officers spent most of their time verifying whether recipients were truthful about their financial and living circumstances. Recipients of Ontario Works were paid monthly benefits that amounted to about 45 percent of the income level at the poverty line or lower. In Ontario, this was defined as the low-income measure.

About 9 percent of urban Ontarians were dependent on this support, with higher percentages in the rural areas and small towns, and 30-plus percent among First Nations. We also knew that those who lived below the poverty line were more likely than other Ontarians to have health problems requiring expensive treatment or long stays in hospitals. The incidence of substance abuse, leaving school at an early age, and trouble with the law was also directly associated with poverty.

In April 2016, prior to my appointment, an all-day roundtable was held to discuss how the government's commitment to a pilot might best be pursued. Keith Banting attended. As mentioned above, he had been the research director for the Macdonald Commission, which had recommended a GAI. By then, he was former director of the Queen's School of Policy Studies. Carolyn Tuohy, former provost of the University of Toronto and a distinguished scholar on comparative health care systems worldwide, attended as well. So did Dr. Danielle Martin, the courageous and outspoken vice-president research at Women's College Hospital in Toronto. A general family practitioner, she was a candid promoter of the single-payer health care system (she had done so to great effect before a US congressional hearing). The roundtable was organized under the auspices of Massey College, Women's College Hospital, and the School of Public Policy and Governance at the University of Toronto. The event brought together people with various views and relevant experience in administering and designing welfare programs or in studying differences in how governments approached poverty abatement. Selected Ontario public servants were there, as were public servants who had worked on the issue with the feds over the years. At the roundtable, the proponents of a basic income reform were balanced by individuals from both the left and the right who disliked the idea of a GAI to begin with. The government knew that understanding the opposition to this innovation would be vital to designing a pilot that provided evidence on key issues of relative cost, measurable benefits to the whole economy, and possible impacts of replacing one system with another.

As a co-chair of the roundtable, I found the day-long discussion robust and thoughtful. It was not without sharp disagreement, but the room was awash in helpful insight and productive discussion about the challenges any pilot would have to address. The roundtable's conclusions were shared with the Province and made available to the public via the website of the School of Public Policy and Governance.

Most fascinating to me that day were the shape and scope of the opposition to any GAI program. The opposition was three-fold. First, those who have worked on solutions to poverty are pragmatic in disposition and granular in their understanding of how our social support systems work federally and provincially. Some of them sincerely believe that a high-profile basic income innovation would be counterproductive. They argue that a mix of nuanced programs – some focused on the aged, some on children, some on people with disabilities, some on training, and so on – will be more effective than a big-bang reform that encourages intense ideological debate.

Another school of opposition comes from the traditional left, whose proponents support carefully designed service programs that are well run by competent public servants. They worry that an automatic top-up, even if more generous, will obviate the need for civil servants and could be used by those on the extreme right to shut down such programs altogether. Some members of this school think that reducing transit fees and increasing affordable government-run housing would be wiser than providing a basic income. (My personal strong bias is in ensuring that everyone is topped up to a livable basic income. This respects the rights of all citizens, even the most disadvantaged, to make their own life choices.)

The third school of opposition holds to what it sees as an inevitable conclusion: if you pay people not to work, they won't. And, of course, the classic bugaboo of the right – "We can't afford it" – always hovers in the air.

All of these negatives were articulately advanced during the round-table, as were other challenges related to the project's design, organization, and guiding purpose.

After my appointment as special advisor on basic income was announced by the minister of community and social services and the premier, Maripier Isabelle and I embarked on the work together. During June, July, and August, we met with provincial officials in various ministries and their counterparts in Ottawa from the Privy Council Office, Statistics Canada, Human Resources and Skills Development Canada, and Finance to examine the critical areas of evidence and the available data sets that would need to be accessed if a pilot were to be meaningful. We met with advocates from various areas that were fundamental to poverty abatement, including housing, food security, education, and support for people with disabilities. We had over a hundred consultations, either in person or by conference call, during a ten-week period. This included meetings with Ontario cabinet committees, municipal leaders, and regional government representatives; health and education practitioners; and, above all, people with ongoing experience of poverty.

We also met with the Opposition party leadership in the Ontario legislature to explain the purposes of the three-year test and to seek its input. PC leader Patrick Brown and NDP leader Andrea Horwath set aside their understandable cynicism about the Liberal government and agreed to await the results of the pilot before levelling any judgment or criticism. Until the summer of 2018, following the election of Progressive Conservative Doug Ford as Ontario premier, all three parties honourably kept this commitment.

In mid-July of 2016, I retreated to Charleston Lake and began assembling the discussion paper for the Province. The paper needed to lay out the reasons for the pilot, identify the kinds of communities in which it should happen, and present a rationale for who should be eligible (as defined by age and income), how the research should be structured, and what kinds of evidence should be gathered. I wanted it to provide a brief history of basic income ideas, take a measured look at federal, inter-provincial, and municipal dynamics, and address the imperative of working with First Nations and Metis in a fashion that respected the reconciliation framework established by the Province. It would also refer to basic income pilots being undertaken in the Netherlands and Finland. These two programs were testing a universal demogrant, a system in which everyone gets a monthly cheque, with the tax system clawing money back from the better off. For the Ontario pilot, I proposed a negative income tax approach – a program that pays a top-up to people beneath the poverty line – which is quite different.

What I found almost universally among the many people with whom Maripier and I met was a genuine belief that we had the data sets essential to shaping a constructive pilot. This opinion was accompanied by angst that governments would not have the political will to actually try this very different approach.

My discussion paper, *Finding a Better Way,* was submitted at the end of August 2016, and the premier formally launched the pilot in Hamilton in March 2017, with Hamilton, Thunder Bay, and Lindsay as designated test sites and a goal of involving four thousand Ontario residents. That the Province accepted my recommendation to double the monthly sum from $640 to $1,300 and to increase the allocation for disabled participants from $1,200 to $1,700 was most encouraging.

With the official launch, my formal role in the Ontario Basic Income Pilot came to an end. But my commitment to basic income as a way of defeating poverty remained, of course, and I awaited the results of the pilot with great interest. I believe firmly that the core freedoms from want and from fear, essential to any society's prospects, as well as to global peace and security, are best preserved when a basic income for all, supportive of work and human dignity, is an integral part of our mixed-market capitalist societies. The infrastructure of roads, highways, schools, airports, and hospitals can and should be buttressed by an infrastructure of civility that gives everyone a chance.

In June 2018, Ontario held a provincial election. During the lead-up to voting day, when asked by the *Toronto Star* whether a Ford government would support the pilot, a senior spokesperson for the Ford campaign confirmed the party's previous position of supporting the pilot to its conclusion on two separate occasions. Christine Elliott, deputy leader of the party and runner-up to Doug Ford for the leadership, indicated the same support. Yet on July 31, 2018, Premier Ford's community services minister, Lisa MacLeod, announced the premature cancellation of the program at barely the one-year mark of a three-year commitment. Ford had campaigned on a slogan of "For the people." Obviously, this didn't extend to low-income people.

CHAPTER 15

Courage and Fairness Matter

▼

Two nations between whom there is no
intercourse and no sympathy; who are as ignorant
of each other's habits, thoughts, and feelings as if
they were dwellers in different zones, or inhabitants
of different planets. The rich and the poor.

BENJAMIN DISRAELI

▲

SIMPLY PUT, MY LIFE experience has shown me that poverty is a cause of
much of the dysfunction that our societies need to address. It is not rocket
science to figure out that someone can live a better life at 70 percent of
the poverty line than at 45 percent, or that a basic income design that
encourages work will be more helpful for a dynamic and growing society
than a welfare regime that discourages it.

The very essence of civility in a free and democratic society is the
general determination never to settle for inequities that can be construct-
ively addressed. The debate about why, how, when, where, and how much
is central to how we move ahead, and sometimes our progress may be
slowed by conflicting views. Working through those disagreements is the
honourable way to proceed, especially when reducing the massive costs

of poverty's pathologies is the ultimate goal. The only unacceptable option is failing to try.

I have done my best in these pages to recount the incidents in my life that shaped my views and prejudices, from the ups and downs of my childhood to my reasoned advocacy for a basic income guarantee in the more than half a century that followed. Since the beginning, my conservatism has been based on a championing of human rights. It has never been about cuddling up to a self-satisfied establishment. Rather, and pointedly, it involves standing apart from the complacent establishment and opposing it when necessary. Any establishment that looks the other way on poverty does not merit support. Inclusive conservatism is the only kind with genuine social and economic relevance.

I have written elsewhere about my view of Canadian conservatism, with its unique attributes, serious flaws, and enduring strengths, particularly in my book *The Right Balance: Canada's Conservative Tradition* (Douglas and McIntyre, 2011). I took a healthy run at the narrowness and selfish self-reverence of neoliberal and neoconservative excess in my book *Beyond Greed: A Traditional Conservative Confronts Neoconservative Excess* (Stoddart, 1997). My concern for the erosion of the best societal and community-embracing views of conservatism in favour of the shallow, selfish myopia that masqueraded as conservatism has been consistent.

Reforming welfare so that those in need are topped up financially and thereby encouraged to work and improve their circumstances without being judged, demeaned, diminished, or micromanaged by the "swells" who work in various overseeing government departments strikes me as the ultimate liberating and uplifting conservative instrument. Who gets support would be a private matter between the Canada Revenue Agency and each citizen. In such a program, the economic mainstream could be broadened, productivity could be encouraged, and the self-respect and community standing of every citizen could be sustained. When government facilitates and establishes such a framework, individuals have the freedom to make their own decisions. I see this as entirely consistent with Tory goals. Not a toy box for all people, but the right for all to work and aspire to own their own toy box and to have one for their children.

▼

Broad interest in basic income experiments has prompted the development of pilot projects around the world. The pilots currently under way in Holland (three cities), Kenya and California. They are also being re-initiated in Finland, as well as being planned by an all-party legislative committee in PEI and studied by a commission in BC. All are structured a little differently, some done by government, some by the private sector. But as they begin to bear fruit, they will generate hard evidence about costs, benefits, and measurable outcomes in terms of social stability and economic opportunity. I have no doubt this evidence will demonstrate that a basic income program in a democracy can generate more genuine help, an increased incentive to work, and less waste, bureaucracy, and stigma than inadequate and overly rules-based welfare programs now provide.

Sadly, during its early days in office, the Progressive Conservative government of Doug Ford chose not to address poverty humanely and efficiently. Instead, it ended the basic income pilot, leaving thousands anxious and uncertain. Those whom the Province had encouraged to sign up for the project were thrown into financial disarray. The decision signals Ontario's move away from innovation and social policy initiatives that had typified the province on education, health care, support for seniors, labour force development, and a host of other areas under Progressive Conservative governments since 1943. The cancellation of the basic income pilot says more about the government in power and the ministers who acquiesced in this backslide than it does about a province where individuals, communities, local organizations, and companies remain committed to finding a better way ahead. These groups are not prepared to settle for a welfare regime that stigmatizes, judges, and entangles people in perpetual poverty or one that discourages work and devalues the dignity and self-respect of so many of their fellow citizens. Shaping economic and social policy before the evidence is in represents a throwback to the kind of authoritarianism that both Conservatives and conservatives have always sought to oppose.

The oft-repeated invocation about seeking the courage to change what can be changed, the serenity to accept what cannot be changed, and the wisdom to know the difference strikes me as an invitation to passivity and an embrace of complacency about the nature of life. Democracy moves forward only when women and men of goodwill refuse to accept injustice, especially when they themselves or people they love are not among the oppressed. An "I'm alright, Jack" bias that leaves too much space for the cruel vicissitudes of life or the excesses of the unmoderated marketplace is not only unfair but deeply harmful to the most serious driving force in any productive society: hope.

Hope is a central commodity in a free, open, and mixed-market economy. Investors invest, entrepreneurs take risks, young people study for degrees and certification, farmers plant and irrigate, traders buy and sell, bankers lend money, and depositors put their earnings in banks, all in the hope that their time, effort, and resources will be rewarded, not perfectly, not always evenly, but by and large fairly.

We have built into our social and economic infrastructure a series of rules and buttresses that sustain hope by constraining the most extreme risks. Canadians have a government guarantee for funds they deposit in certified financial institutions. Farmers can have crop insurance backstopped by the government. We have tough regulation on full financial disclosure so that investors can understand the risks they are trying to navigate. In other words, hope is not a free-standing virtue, unsubsidized or unsupported by the community. It is a product of explicit public and regulatory policy.

Hope emerges for everyday citizens when societies act rationally to preserve the two freedoms that matter most – freedom from want and freedom from fear. For totalitarians of the right or the left, the latter is most frightening. By its very nature, it dilutes the ability of a terrorist state to control and intimidate. Freedom from want enables people to anticipate a better life, to care well for their families and neighbours, and to embrace hard work as a way of gradually moving up the ladder to enjoy better lives with their families and communities.

During my own youthful, if not terribly unique, exposure to poverty, and in the years since, I have watched heavy waves swamp the working poor, spoken with distressed unemployed people who no longer qualify for employment insurance, and witnessed the despair among First Nations, inner-city, and rural folks caught in downward cycles not of their own making. This has taught me never to underestimate the desperation and anger that sustained poverty can generate for a family, a neighbourhood, a city, or a country.

In Canada, people can be poor for many reasons. They may be out of work but ineligible for employment insurance. They may have a physical or intellectual disability, or be recent immigrants or refugees. They may have been laid off from work and are too old to find another job but are not yet sixty-five, so they cannot receive the federal guaranteed income supplement. Or they may live in a part of Canada with depressed economic prospects or where traditional industries such as fishing, forestry, and mining have been automated away from labour-intensive practices. It is these factors that have put 3 million or more Canadians beneath the poverty line, not any moral failing on their part. And this number has not changed meaningfully in decades.

We know without question that poverty is the best predictor of poor health outcomes, the early development of chronic illness, increased hospitalization and chance of imprisonment, family breakup, family violence, and school drop-out rates that in themselves lead to lower earning prospects. Not acting to address the problem directly borders on the criminal.

In Kingston, Ontario, there are seven prisons within a hundred miles of the city centre. Eighty percent of their inmates come from the less than 15 percent of our national population who live beneath the poverty line. The average cost for sustaining one prisoner is anywhere from $45,000 to $150,000 annually, depending on the level of security required. Most Canadians could be lifted out of poverty for less than $1,000 a month.

Poverty is the thief of time. Individuals who are severely stressed by a basic lack of liquidity and are scrambling to make ends meet do not have enough time to be involved parents, caring volunteers, good neighbours, or contributing members of their community, though many poor people manage these things anyway.

In Canada's 2011 federal election, the issue of poverty did not come up once in the CBC TV national leadership debate moderated by the bright, fair, and affable Steve Paikin. When I asked him why that was, he patiently explained, "Hugh, we do extensive voter research to determine which questions Canadians want asked of the party leaders, and frankly, poverty wasn't mentioned."

John Kenneth Galbraith's iconic 1992 essay "The Culture of Contentment" documents in plain language how politics has become about only the better off. Political parties and candidates cater to those who engage, participate, vote, and donate. At first glance, this might be understandable, but it also excludes the poorest among us. Poverty steals many things from its victims: good health, opportunity, stability, community, and, as noted, time above all else – such as the time to respond to a research poll. A national TV debate involving all registered party leaders in which the word "poverty" is never uttered speaks eloquently to this harsh exclusionary reality.

Canada already helps citizens through universal health insurance, old-age pensions, and free primary and secondary education. These are all efforts in the right direction. Across world democracies, tax dollars are spent on these pillars of support because it is good for the economy overall. Why are we not prepared on a national basis to guarantee an annual income to those who fall beneath the poverty line? We extend taxpayer-funded liquidity to big institutions that face collapse because of exogenous costs, unavoidable misfortune, or their own bad judgment. But when it comes to individuals, we extend tiny, hard-to-extract, excessively bureaucratic sums that do not even come close to lifting them back into the economic mainstream.

Political parties across the country have expressed their support for guaranteed annual income policies. At their 2016 convention, the federal Liberals adopted a resolution that asked their party "to develop a poverty reduction strategy aimed at providing a minimum guaranteed income" by working in collaboration with the provinces and territories. The federal Greens and New Democrats have also adopted resolutions supporting a GAI policy. In 2016, leaders from the four main political parties of Prince Edward Island welcomed initiatives on a GAI. Since the new Progressive Conservative minority government was elected in 2019 an all-party approach to planning a Secure Income Pilot project has been initiated. The Liberals and the Greens in Manitoba, and the New Democrats in Saskatchewan and Nova Scotia, have also expressed support for such programs. Various Senate reports in Canada, from the 1970s to 2013, have called for either a GAI or nation-wide pilots to test its prospective benefits and costs. By reducing poverty and thereby the pathologies that affect the poor, a core GAI program may well produce a return on investment that is equal to or better than the cost of the program.

In the spring of 2018, the parliamentary budget officer reported a net cost of $43 billion annually of a basic income top-up at the national level of the kind that was briefly tested in Ontario. That did not count the yearly savings to the provinces from no-longer-necessary provincial welfare and disability programs, which are worth approximately $10 billion annually in Ontario alone. This brings the price of eradicating poverty and all its extra costs down to approximately 10 percent of federal annual on-and-off balance sheet expenditures. This is a small price to pay for an investment in genuine equality of opportunity.

The Organisation for Economic Co-operation and Development has generated numbers on levels of poverty and their impact on productivity and economic growth abroad. And the United Nations has produced numbers on the links between violence and poverty in many countries. Their takeaway message could not be clearer. The weakening of either of the two freedoms (from fear or from want) puts the other in peril. When hope is snuffed out for some but remains supple for others, that imbalance is always a predictor of trouble on the horizon.

What would the gains be in Asia, Europe, and Africa if the basic income tests being run in many parts of the world gave politicians, especially finance ministers, the clarity of purpose to put poverty eradication first? How many global areas of tension would be calmed? Where might we be if, for example, the middle-income residents of Gaza earned better than one-fourteenth of the neighbouring lowest-income Israelis? As I've argued, income security and strategic security are linked inextricably, and in the beginning and in the end, they are about hope. Where hope exists, and is justified, terrorism and violence have little to offer.

The road to basic, affordable, and engaged economic opportunity for the poor in Canada is still a steep incline. But the battle has not ended. For those who signed up in good faith for the Ontario Basic Income Pilot and have now been so cruelly disappointed, the Ford government's decision is beyond tragic. Its actions will not be forgotten by people of any – or no – political stripe. Governments have often chosen to tinker at the margins in relation to poverty, improving inadequate programs by increments and continuing the bureaucratic bias toward government command and control of the lives of poor people. Those on the far right and the far left, as well as members of the "bureaucracy knows best" subgroup, may rejoice at this turn in the road, at this detour from evidence-based assessment of what could work better. But bad public policy sustained by narrow politicians rarely has a good chance of survival. Change may be put off, and proceeding with greater humanity and logic can be postponed. But the trend toward economic fairness cannot be eradicated. Should this ever occur, the very balance and viability of our mixed-market economy will be in peril – with all the political fallout that will generate.

This is all a very long way from the burning of my mahogany toy box in Monsieur Lacroix's empty furnace almost six decades ago. My wife recently reminded me that, as our friends started their families over the years, our gift to them was always a toy box. Until now, I hadn't realized the significance of that.

I am no longer angry at my dad. The toy box was all that he had to help a neighbour whose economic straits were even more dire than ours. I have forgiven you, Dad. In your place at the great cab stand in heaven, I hope you will chuckle at how long it took me to admit it. My father did the right thing. We all need to do the right thing now.

Reflections on the Ontario Basic Income Pilot

Launched in March 2017 by the Liberal government of Kathleen Wynne, the Ontario Basic Income Pilot involved four thousand participants, replacing their welfare and disability support with an automatic cash top-up tied to income. Based in the towns of Thunder Bay, Hamilton, and Lindsay, it was an experiment, and its purpose and nature were not grounded in advocacy. How well would replacing the traditional forms of social assistance work out? Would it be less stigmatizing for recipients? Would it ultimately cost more, even though it diminished the numbers of poor people and thus generated savings in health care and other services?

What should the right top-up level be? How would its recipients fare in comparison to a similar group on welfare? On this score, the discussion paper titled *Finding a Better Way,* which was published by the Province in August 2017, made no assumptions (for the paper itself, see https://www.ontario.ca/page/finding-better-way-basic-income-pilot-project-ontario). It laid out a clear analysis of the actual costs of poverty to Ontario, including and beyond the roughly $10 billion per year being shelled out through Ontario Works (welfare) and the Ontario Disability Support Program (ODSP).

Although the pilot was intended to run for three years, with first payment distributed in October 2017, it was cancelled in July 2018, before one-third of its test period had elapsed, shortly after the Doug Ford Progressive Conservatives unseated the Liberals at Queen's Park. The new government claimed that the pilot was unaffordable, but this was simply the narrow ideology of fact-free analysis talking. After barely a third of the trial period, the data would simply not have been sufficient to make that determination.

Had the pilot been permitted to run its course, it could have provided valuable information with which to shape social policy. For example, it might have improved workplace participation rates. In most provinces, traditional welfare discourages recipients from seeking paid employment. If they earn an extra hundred or two hundred dollars a month, their welfare benefits are clawed back dollar-for-dollar. This policy is an obvious disincentive to work. By contrast, the basic income pilot encouraged employment, with a taxation level that made working worthwhile. Pilot participants whose employment income equalled the amount of the top-up grant paid the same tax rate as other Canadians. The ability to measure how this approach increased workplace participation and strengthened the labour force was lost when the program was cancelled.

The pilot might also have upgraded educational achievement. Low-income households typically have negative educational outcomes. Young people drop out of school, imperilling their long-term career prospects. Being a single parent on Ontario Works does not facilitate educational engagement. The top-up supplied by the basic income pilot allowed recipients to go back to school.

And finally, the pilot could have positively affected both individuals and communities. During the mid-1970s, the federal and Manitoba governments launched their Mincome project in Dauphin, Manitoba, to experiment with a guaranteed income. Evelyn Forget painstakingly analyzed its results, tracking not only what happened to individual Mincome participants (in terms of health status, labour force connection, education) but also what happened in Dauphin itself, as well as in other Manitoba communities.

The 2017 basic income pilot was structured to do the same in Ontario, with individual outcomes measured in the three very different communities of Thunder Bay, Hamilton, and Lindsay. These towns had different economic bases, a different demographic mix, and unique attributes that were reflective of their regions. Their size also enabled community effects to be measured, such as participation in community life, volunteerism, school attendance, collective levels of health care use, and policing. Clearly, any rational assessment of the community and fiscal costs and benefits of a basic income replacement for welfare and the ODSP would benefit from this kind of overall combination. Scrapping the project meant that no assessment of individual or community impacts, good, bad, or indifferent, would take place at all.

Evidence-based versus ideology-based social policy has been distressingly rare over the last few decades in North America. Governments often fiddle with the design of a program, basing their approach on anecdotal or field office comment rather than any hard data on behaviour, fiscal costs, or measurable return on investment for the public funds deployed. A case in point is Ontario's expensive photo ID health card, introduced due to the perceived increase in fraudulent use of the old card. However, this perception was never measured by hard data, and in fact the fraud levels were very similar to those for consumer credit cards. But the political masters of the day were under pressure to "look tough," which was all the data they needed to implement the costly change.

Ontario's basic income pilot was structured to generate hard data for the public domain. Its costs and benefits would be compared to those of the welfare program and ODSP. The overall planning document, *Finding a Better Way,* was clear that no assumptions were being made about how the dollars, costs, relative benefits, and impact on marginal tax rates would play out. The purpose of the pilot was to get objective data-based answers to address many of the shibboleths, both positive and negative, about welfare reform. Those data would have been professionally tabulated, made widely available, and delivered openly to the legislature, media, and Ontario residents, for all to see and decide upon. This fact partially explains the support that the pilot received from the Opposition parties, the Conference Board, municipal leaders, and the various public health, medical, social work, and community organizations. Setting this aside in favour of an ideologically driven cancellation in a fact-free context speaks only to the angst that some conservatives and, sadly, some bureaucrats feel about attempting change.

The pilot might also have enabled the government to kick its path-dependency habit. In path dependency, governments move back and forth along the same path in a policy area. They may vary their speed or tilt (a bit to the right or the left), but they never set off in a new direction. Over time, the path becomes a rut, and the sun and the light recede into the distance. Far too many government programs, on prisons, immigration, poverty abatement, or the treatment of seniors, fall into this category worldwide, not just in Canada. Our level of genuine experimentation in social policy is abysmal. Fortunately, our health practitioners and researchers have been wildly more courageous and innovative. Had they not stepped into the breach, very few of us could expect to live beyond our early sixties.

The outcomes of the pilot would also have helped government to understand that poverty is a cause of misery, not a result of it. People on the right often prescribe "bootstraps" to those who lack boots, and many on the left prefer well-staffed government programs that treat low-income individuals as clients rather than citizens. Both camps love to hide behind the "poverty is complex" argument. "There are many causes of poverty," they say, "such as immigration status, disabilities, bad parenting, illiteracy, marital breakup, and the rest. Poverty is a result of many things we cannot fix." This form of logic acts as a shield against change, ensuring that nothing meaningful will be attempted. It is sustained by the notion that not even the wealthiest of states could find enough cash to fix all of the contributing factors.

As I have argued elsewhere, when an accident victim is wheeled into a trauma ward, the front-line medical staff don't begin their urgent care by asking the patient to fill out a questionnaire on diet and exercise or educational background. They begin by stopping the bleeding and stabilizing the patient's vital signs. People who can't afford to pay their rent, put food on the table, buy warm clothes, or purchase a transit pass need a transfusion of cash right away. Of course, analytical work on how they can improve their medium- and long-term prospects is important. But first, the transfusion. The basic income pilot was intended to achieve just that – to top up low-income Ontarians from 45 percent of the poverty line to 75 percent. And, unlike normal welfare, it would have provided a genuine incentive to work. In other words, the pilot would have tested how treating poverty as a cause of low educational status, poor health, unemployment, loneliness, and substance abuse might work, in comparison to the present dysfunctional approach. The latter simply helps people to live within poverty and offers no stepladder to full membership in the economic mainstream. The cancellation of the pilot cements Ontario into the pits of this dysfunction, with little upside for low-income Ontarians.

Valuable scientific analysis shaped by rigorous research, on the one hand, and community and media engagement, on the other, was one of the compelling benefits being produced by the pilot beyond the hard data. Senior government officials, academic researchers from various universities, community advocacy and support groups, volunteers from a range of organizations, and observers from other provinces and countries were all keenly involved in support of the Ontarians who were enrolled in the pilot. Its cancellation ended that community endeavour. And this, after the government's public promise that the pilot would be allowed to continue.

As I reflected on that broken promise, its timing, and the utter lack of even the most minimal consultation with pilot participants, it occurred to me that the cancellation, abrupt and surprising as it was, sounded a warning. It was really the first loud chirp from a canary in distress in the mineshaft of Ontario politics circa 2018.

Clearly, the Ford government is not a Progressive Conservative government. It does not espouse the policy balance and traditions that typified Ontario PC governments since the election of Premier George Drew's minority in 1943 right through to the Frank Miller government that was defeated by Liberal David Peterson in 1985. Although none of these governments were perfect, some having scandal problems and policy snafus, all were committed to broadening the economic mainstream. They were committed to improving the prospects for low-income Ontarians of all ages. Thus, they invested in education, made post-secondary education financially accessible to more young Ontarians, welcomed newcomers (including asylum seekers), and established innovative outreach instruments such as TVOntario and the Ontario Institute for Studies in Education. They created provincial initiatives to facilitate homeownership, broadened agricultural crop insurance, and installed rent controls that sought to be fair to both tenants and landlords. During the 1980s, they founded centres of excellence for the automotive and food industries, pharmaceuticals, agriculture, and computing science.

In other words, Progressive Conservatives in Ontario looked forward and were not always prisoners of the past. One of the secrets here was leadership renewal – embracing a coming generation of leaders as opposed to reaching back. Hence, John Parmenter Robarts, who advanced infrastructure and post-secondary expansion to address the needs of baby boomers and who embraced the universal health insurance proposals coming from Saskatchewan. Hence, Bill Davis, who stopped the Spadina Expressway expansion, tilting toward the Jane Jacobs view of the value of neighbourhoods, parks, and communities, and who ended up being an architect of the Canadian Charter of Rights and Freedoms, French-language services in Ontario, and the guaranteed income supplement for seniors. He was elected premier four times, serving in the post for fourteen years.

The present leadership has limited roots in the Progressive Conservative Party, beyond having a parent who served honourably in the legislature. Campaigning on a "For the people" slogan, as Doug Ford did, capitalized on the broad desire for change after fifteen years of Liberal rule.

But in turning away from a young, new-generation leader, who had brought a broad multicultural presence to the city-side of what is usually a small-town and rural base, the PC Party made a serious mistake. Patrick Brown wasn't even allowed twenty-four hours to try and clear his name from allegations of troubling behaviour. And the subsequent leadership campaign and vote were not above serious scrutiny. When the Ford administration was launched, few people, even within the party, had any idea of what its priorities were. A con-trived $15 billion annual deficit, unsophisticated meddling in publicly traded Hydro, which produced the loss of a multi-billion-dollar asset acquisition, a chimera of nothing on promises regarding "a buck a beer," the senseless downgrading of French-language services, the cancellation of a minimum wage increase and labour standards reforms all spoke to a narrow, hard-right extremism that was totally outside the mainstream of Ontario PC Party pol-itics and government. Populism that is about resentment, envy, cronyism, and the very denial of cabinet government, imposing one-man rule in which min-isters are not permitted to run their own portfolios, let alone contribute to government decision making, is a very thin pane of glass, with zero weight-bearing capacity. This is especially true after the post-election honeymoon has waned and complex problems and strong public feedback begin to crest. "For the people" should include all the people.

I know and like many of the ministers and MPPs in the new Ford government and wish them well personally. But to date, their input, along with that of other ministers and MPPs, has been either unwelcome or lacking in consequence.

Cabinet solidarity after reaching a decision is one thing; having no chance to influence the decision before it is reached is another. This goes beyond right, left, or centre. It goes directly to process, inclusion, and the right of ministers to have their say. After all, their oath of allegiance is to the Crown, not to the premier or his staff.

The surprise cancellation of the Ontario Basic Income Pilot was indeed the canary in the coal mine.

Acknowledgments

Although every book has an author or co-authors, most books that cover a broad range in time, locales, and circumstances have many who contributed to the author's understanding, learning, and focus.

I am very grateful to Barbara Pulling, my copy editor at UBC Press. Her sense of coherence, logic, linkage, and textual integrity made a very serious difference in the quality of this effort. Holly Keller, the production manager, with great patience brought an integrated sense of context to the assembly of the book itself. Randy Schmidt, the editor for political and policy books at UBC Press, was extraordinary in his encouragement, advice, guidance, and broad sensibility for the story I wanted to tell and how best to convey its salience to readers.

Rosemarie Brisson graciously set aside her weekends and holidays to help with the typing and reorganization of my chapters. Her razor sharp memory of events and the battles we fought together over the years was invaluable as both a muse, a de facto content editor, and a memory prompt. Above all, she was a friend, who gave me the bad news and the good as necessary, rarely sugar-coating any of it. Keith Banting, Lowell Murray, and Graham Scott were present when Robert Stanfield embraced the basic income concept, and they attended the conferences at Little Whitefish Lake and Niagara that moved the idea along. They joined David MacDonald, my first employer, in helping to connect dots and sentences and important historical threads.

To my colleagues in the Senate, especially Senators Art Eggleton, Joyce Fairbairn, and Nancy Ruth, and to clerks of committees, such as François Michaud and Barbara Reynolds, who helped with the committee work that meant so much, a special tip of the hat.

To Evelyn Forget, whose courage and leadership on the methodological challenges of assessing what happened at the Mincome project, no thanks on my part could ever be enough. Her special mix of modesty, diligence, academic integrity, and courage has been simply invaluable.

To Maripier Isabelle, now an assistant professor of economics at l'Université Laval after completing postdoctoral research in Paris, my most respectful and sincere gratitude. Her methodological coherence and rigour, indomitable spirit, and drive made my modest work on the file possible.

At Massey College, my colleagues on the staff, and the governing board members who allowed me to accept the pro-bono assignment with the Province, all deserve special credit and appreciation. I want to say an extra word of thanks to Sarah Moritz, the college assistant, Elena Ferranti, her successor, and my colleague Amela Marin, the college dean of fellowships, who helped and supported in many ways too numerous to mention.

Although the ability to put together an effort like this is the product of many genuinely helpful and thoughtful fellow travellers, any mistakes or mischaracterizations are mine alone.

Donna Armstrong Segal, my life partner of over forty years, and Jacqueline Sadye Armstrong Segal, our daughter, help every day in ways too private, emotional, and nuanced to adequately describe. Suffice it to say, they are the reason I have the will and desire to keep on keeping on.

Charleston Lake
Leeds County
Ontario

Selected Bibliography

Over time, countless factors shape our views, biases, and strongly held opinions. Some of the factors in my life are the people and events I have tried to describe honourably in these fifteen chapters. But I would be less than frank if I dismissed the influence of written works in my evolution and deepening of conviction on how best to eradicate poverty, including works on global security, human and economic rights, peace, order, and good government.

The works in this bibliography are offered, not with the intent of convincing or advocating a certain position, but simply to track the many sources of the policy bias that I have embraced. They are respectfully offered in the full knowledge that readers may have their own opinions about basic income and equality of opportunity. Having read the works listed here, they will reach their own conclusions, which may differ from mine.

Informed debate based on evidence, logic, passion, and views is never a bad thing. Poverty is a central challenge for modern mixed-market economies and democracies such as those in Canada, the European Union, the United States, Africa, and Asia. For anyone who is interested in the issue, reading the views of others from prior times, present contexts, and emergent analytics is a good place to begin or to continue learning. The works listed here are not the only sources of insight, analysis, or conclusion on the poverty debate, but they are the ones that had the greatest impact on me.

Some take a global and historic perspective, some confine themselves to a certain period in history, some drill down on the discipline of economics, some examine public policy and choices, some look at causes, and some assess outcomes. All contributed to the judgments I reached, the cause I adopted, and the clarity of my perspective on the issue. I have no one but myself to blame for any naiveté, presumption, or undue idealism that may have infected my conclusions or advocacy. I apologize to no one for those flaws, where they exist. But to the extent that the purpose of my engagement has been strengthened by coherence, fact, rational judgment, and evidence, I am delighted to give praise for that strength to the authors and works listed here.

▼

The following deal with the global, domestic, and historical context of poverty, power, and fairness.

Alexandroff, Alan, ed. *Can the World Be Governed? Possibilities for Effective Multilateralism*. Waterloo: Wilfrid Laurier Press, 2008.

Arendt, Hannah. *The Origins of Totalitarianism*. New York: Harcourt Brace Jovanovich, 1976.

Armstrong, Sally. *Bitter Roots, Tender Shoots: The Uncertain Fate of Afghanistan's Women*. Toronto: Viking, 2008.

Bailey, Laura E. "The Impact of Conflict on Poverty." World Bank, Operational Policy and Country Services, Fragile States Unit, Washington, 2006.

Boyko, John. *Bennett: The Rebel Who Challenged and Changed a Nation*. Toronto: Key Porter Books, 2010.

Buzan, Barry. *People, States and Fear: The National Security Problem in International Relations*. Brighton, UK: Wheatsheaf Books, 1983.

Churchill, Winston. *The People's Rights*. London: Hodder and Stoughton, 1909.

Green, E.H.H. *Ideologies of Conservatism: Political Ideas in the Twentieth Century*. New York: Oxford University Press, 2002.

Hedges, Chris. *War Is a Force That Gives Us Meaning*. New York: Anchor Books, 2003.

Hitchens, Christopher. *Love, Poverty and War*. London: Nation Books, 2004.

Marshall, George C. "The Marshall Plan." Speech to Harvard University, June 5, 1947.

Moore, Charles. *Margaret Thatcher: The Authorized Biography*. Vol. 1. London: Allen Laine, 2013.

Piketty, Thomas. *Capital in the Twenty-First Century*. Cambridge, MA: Belknap Press, 2014.

Skelton, O.D. *Our Generation: Its Gains and Losses*. Chicago: University of Chicago Press, 1938.

Smith, Adam. *On the Wealth of Nations*. Vol. 2. Oxford: Clarendon Press, 1869.

Stiglitz, Joseph. *The Price of Inequality*. New York: W.H. Norton, 2013.

Wilkinson, Richard G., and Michael Marmot. *Social Determinants of Health*. Copenhagen: Oxford University Press, 1999.

Wilkinson, Richard, and Kate Pickett. *The Spirit Level: Why Greater Equality Makes Societies Stronger.* London: Allen Lane, 2009.

▼

The following are useful for social and economic policy and for conditions in North and South America.

Battle, K., and S. Torjman. *Breaking Down the Welfare Wall.* Ottawa: Caledon Institute of Social Policy, 1993.

Canadian Institute of Advanced Research and Health Canada, Population and Public Health Branch. "Social Determinants of Health." Ottawa, 2002.

Carty, R. Kenneth. *Big Tent Politics: The Liberal Party's Mastery of Canada's Public Life.* Vancouver: UBC Press, 2015.

Copp, Terry. *The Anatomy of Poverty: The Canadian Working Class in Montreal, 1897–1929.* Toronto: McClelland and Stewart.

Courchene, Thomas J. *Social Policy in the 1990s: Agenda for Reform.* Toronto: Prentice Hall, 1978.

Croll, David. *Poverty in Canada: Report of the Special Senate Committee on Poverty.* Ottawa: Information Canada, 1971.

Eggleton, Art. *In from the Margins: A Call to Action on Poverty, Housing and Homelessness.* December 2009. http://publications.gc.ca/collections/collection_2010/parl/YC17-402-2-01-eng.pdf.

Friedman, Milton. *Capitalism and Freedom.* Chicago: University of Chicago Press, 1962.

Frum, David. *Comeback: Conservatism That Can Win Again.* New York: Broadway, 2008.

Guttmann, Astrid. "Child Poverty, Health and Health Care Use in Canada." *Journal of Pediatrics and Child Health* 6, 8 (October 2001): 509–13.

Hellman, A.G. *How Does Bolsa Familia Work?* Washington, DC: Inter-American Development Bank, 2015.

Laube, Aly. "Minimum Guaranteed Income Resolution Passes at Liberal Party Convention." *The Runner,* June 14, 2016.

Martin, Danielle. *Better Now: Six Big Ideas to Improve Health Care for All Canadians.* Toronto: Allen Lane, 2017.

Morgan, Jane. *Conflict and Order: The Police and Labour Disputes, 1900–1939.* London: Oxford University Press, 1987.

Novak, Michael. *The Spirit of Democratic Capitalism.* Lanham: Madison Books, 1982.

OECD. *Society at a Glance, 2016: OECD Social Indicators*. Paris: OECD Publishing, 2016.

Plante, Charles, and Keisha Sharpe. *Poverty Costs Saskatchewan: A New Approach to Prosperity for All*. Saskatoon: Poverty Costs, 2014.

Puxley, Evelyn. *Poverty in Montreal*. Montreal: Dawson College, 1971.

Simeon, Richard. *Federal-Provincial Diplomacy: The Making of Recent Policy in Canada*. Toronto: University of Toronto Press, 1972.

Standing, Guy. *The Precariat: The New Dangerous Class*. London: Bloomsbury, 2011.

Stanfield, Robert. "Policy Making in National Politics." Speech to the Empire Club of Canada, Toronto, October 2, 1969.

Vaïsse, Justin. *Neoconservatism: The Biography of a Movement*. Cambridge, MA: Belknap Press, 2010.

Wilderquist, Karl, and Michael Howard, eds. *Alaska's Permanent Fund Dividend*. New York: Palgrave Macmillan, 2012.

▼

Further reading, which I recommend enthusiastically, especially in terms of acquiring a better understanding of the framework within which policies are shaped and negotiated, includes the following.

Banting, Keith. *Poverty, Politics and Policy: Britain in the 1960s*. London: Palgrave Macmillan, 1979.

–. *The Welfare State and Canadian Federalism*. Montreal and Kingston: McGill-Queen's University Press, 1982.

Banting, Keith, and John Myles. *Inequality and the Fading of Redistributive Politics*. Vancouver: UBC Press, 2015.

Forget, Evelyn. *Basic Income for Canadians*. Toronto: James Lorimer, 2018.

Hughes, Chris. *Fair Shot: Rethinking Inequality and How We Earn*. London: Bloomsbury, 2018.

Moynihan, Daniel P. *The Politics of a Guaranteed Annual Income: The Nixon Administration and the Family Assistance Plan*. New York: Vintage Books, 1973.

Palmer, Bryan, and Gaetan Heroux. *Toronto's Poor: A Rebellious History*. Toronto: Between the Lines Press, 2016.

Pereira, Richard. *The Cost of Universal Basic Income: Public Savings and Programme Redundancy Exceed Costs in Financing Basic Income*. New York: Springer International, 2017.

Raphael, David. *Social Determinants of Health*. 2nd ed. Toronto: Canadian
    Scholars' Press, 2009.
Skidelsky, Robert, and Edward Skidelsky. *How Much Is Enough?* London:
    Penguin, 2012.
Stern, Andy. *Raising the Floor: How a Universal Basic Income Can Renew Our
    Economy and Rebuild the American Dream*. New York: Public Affairs, 2016.

▼

No mix of fifty works is collectively unique or exhaustive or definitive on any
subject, including the struggle against poverty and its impact. These are the
works, past, present, and very new, that have shaped my view of the dynamics
of poverty and of how we can design the much-needed policy to seriously
reduce poverty in our time.

Index

Note: An (i) after a page number indicates an illustration.